This Journal Belongs to

© 2013 by Barbour Publishing, Inc.

Print ISBN 978-1-62416-647-1

All rights reserved. No part of this publication may be reproduced or transmitted for commercial purposes, except for brief quotations in printed reviews, without written permission of the publisher.

"Amazing Grace" is attributed to English poet and clergyman John Newton.

Published by Barbour Publishing, Inc., P.O. Box 719, Uhrichsville, Ohio 44683, www.barbourbooks.com

Our mission is to publish and distribute inspirational products offering exceptional value and biblical encouragement to the masses.

Member of the Evangelical Christian Publishers Association

Printed in China.

Amazing Grace,
how sweet the sound
That saved
a wretch like me,
I once was lost
but now am found,
Was Blind,
but now I see.

— John Newton

Amazing grace, how sweet the sound, That saved a wretch like me!

I once was lost but now am found, *Was blind* but now I see.

> 'Twas grace that taught my heart to fear,
> And grace my fears relieved;

How *precious* did that *grace* appear The hour *I first believed!*

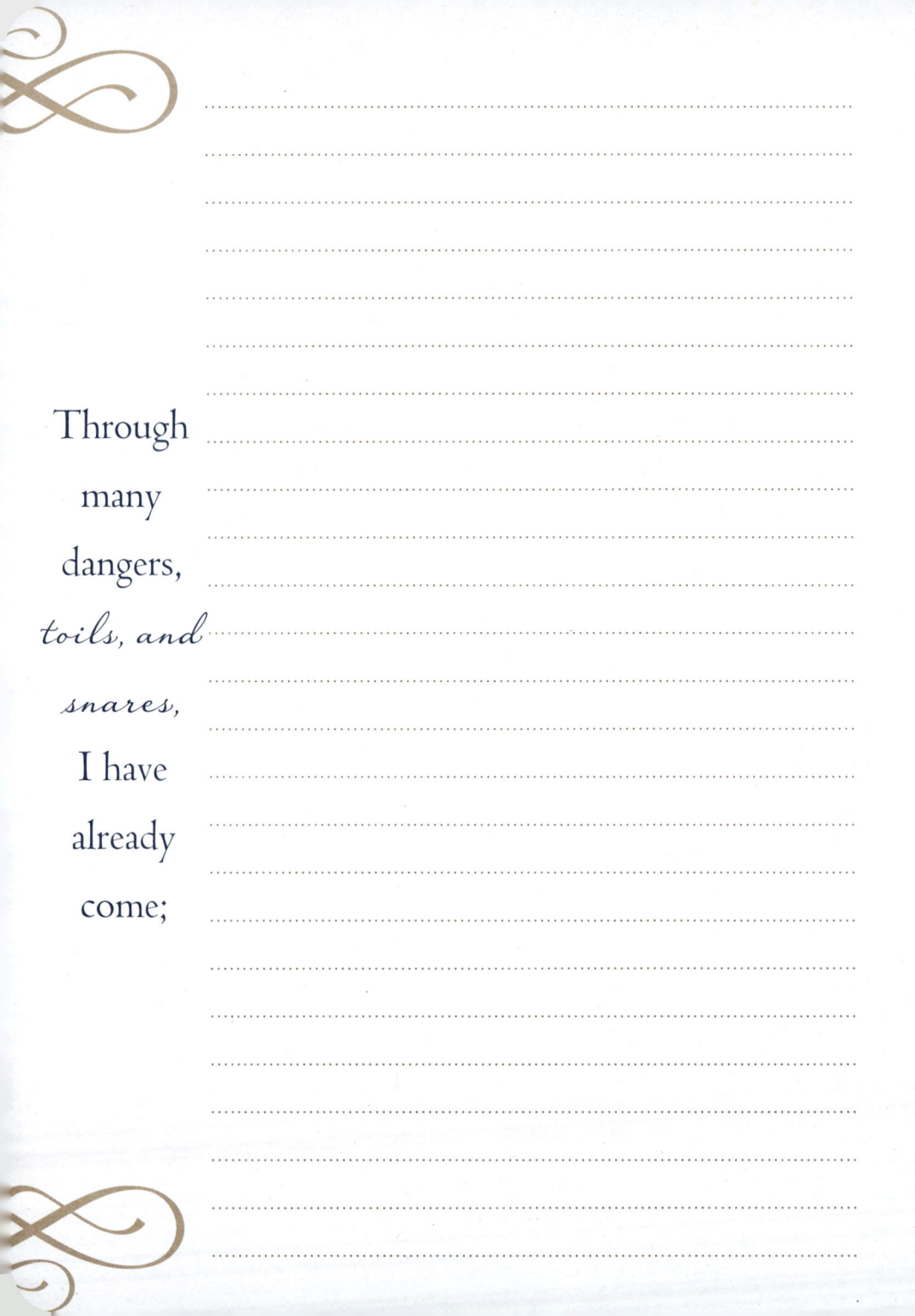

Through many dangers, *toils, and snares,* I have already come;

'Twas *grace* that brought me safe thus far, *And* *grace* will lead me home.

The Lord has promised good to me. His Word my hope secures.

He will my shield and portion be, As long as life endures.

The earth shall soon dissolve like snow, The sun forbear to shine;

But God, who called me here below, Will be forever mine.

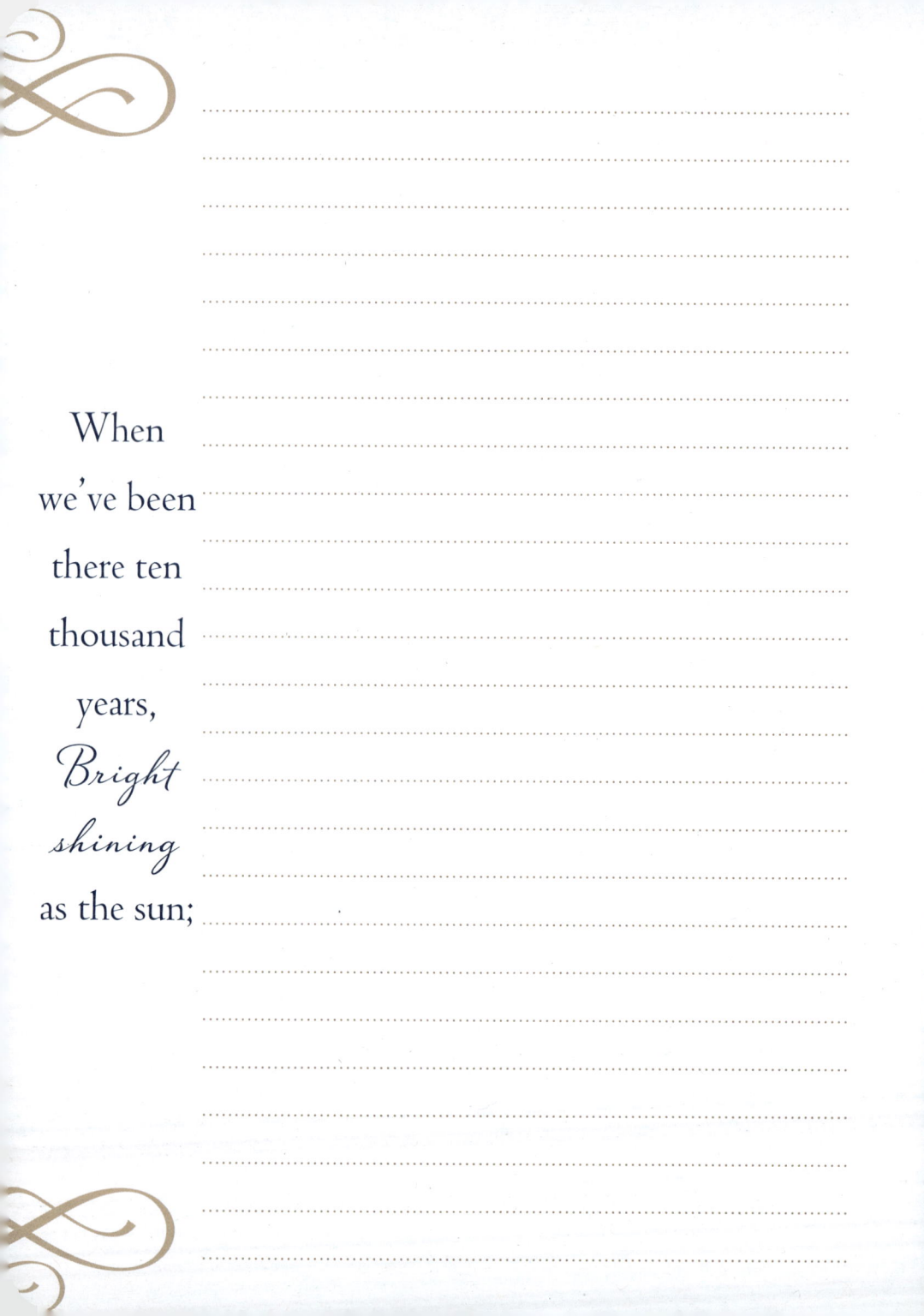

When we've been there ten thousand years,
Bright shining as the sun;

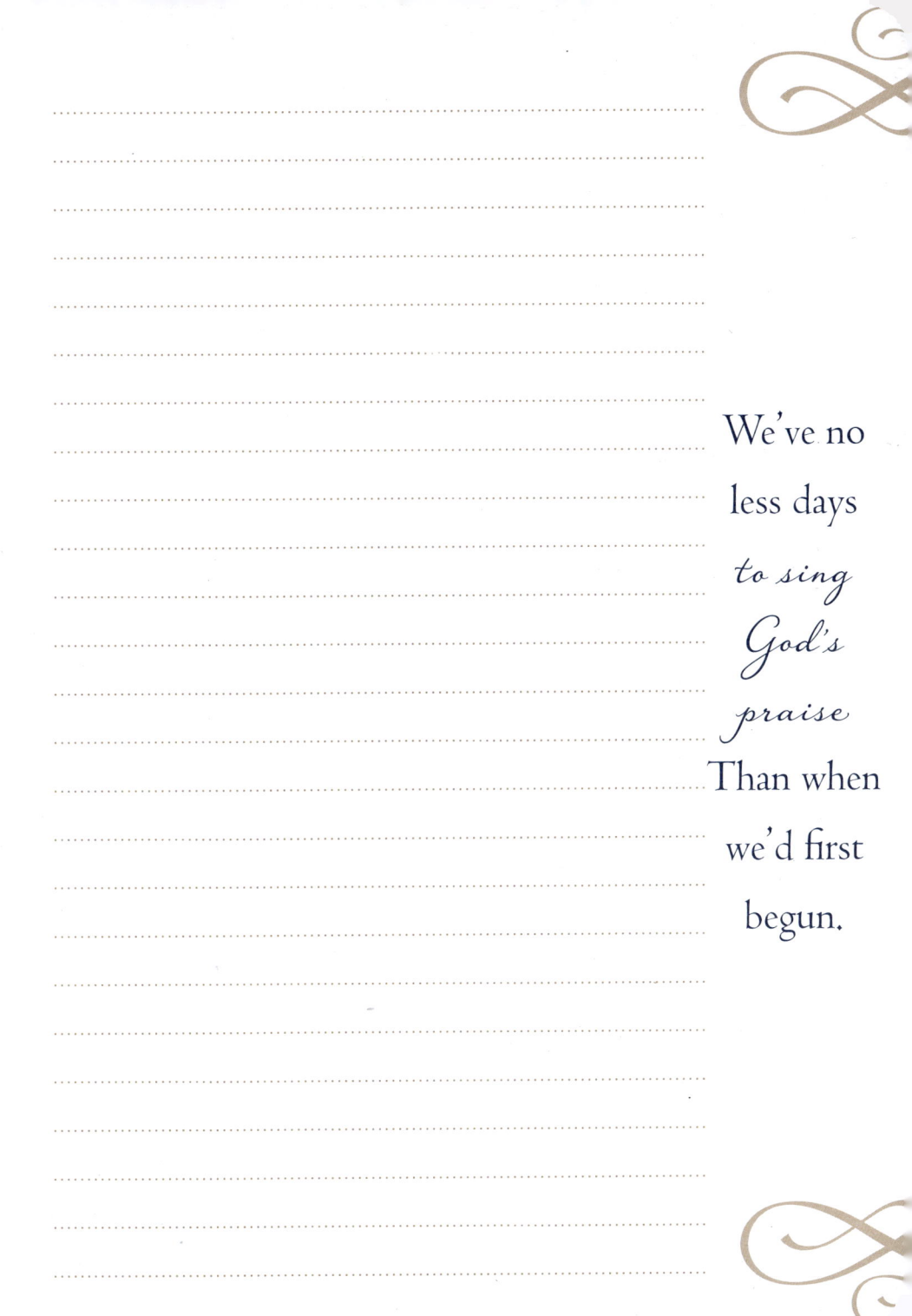

We've no less days *to sing God's praise* Than when we'd first begun.

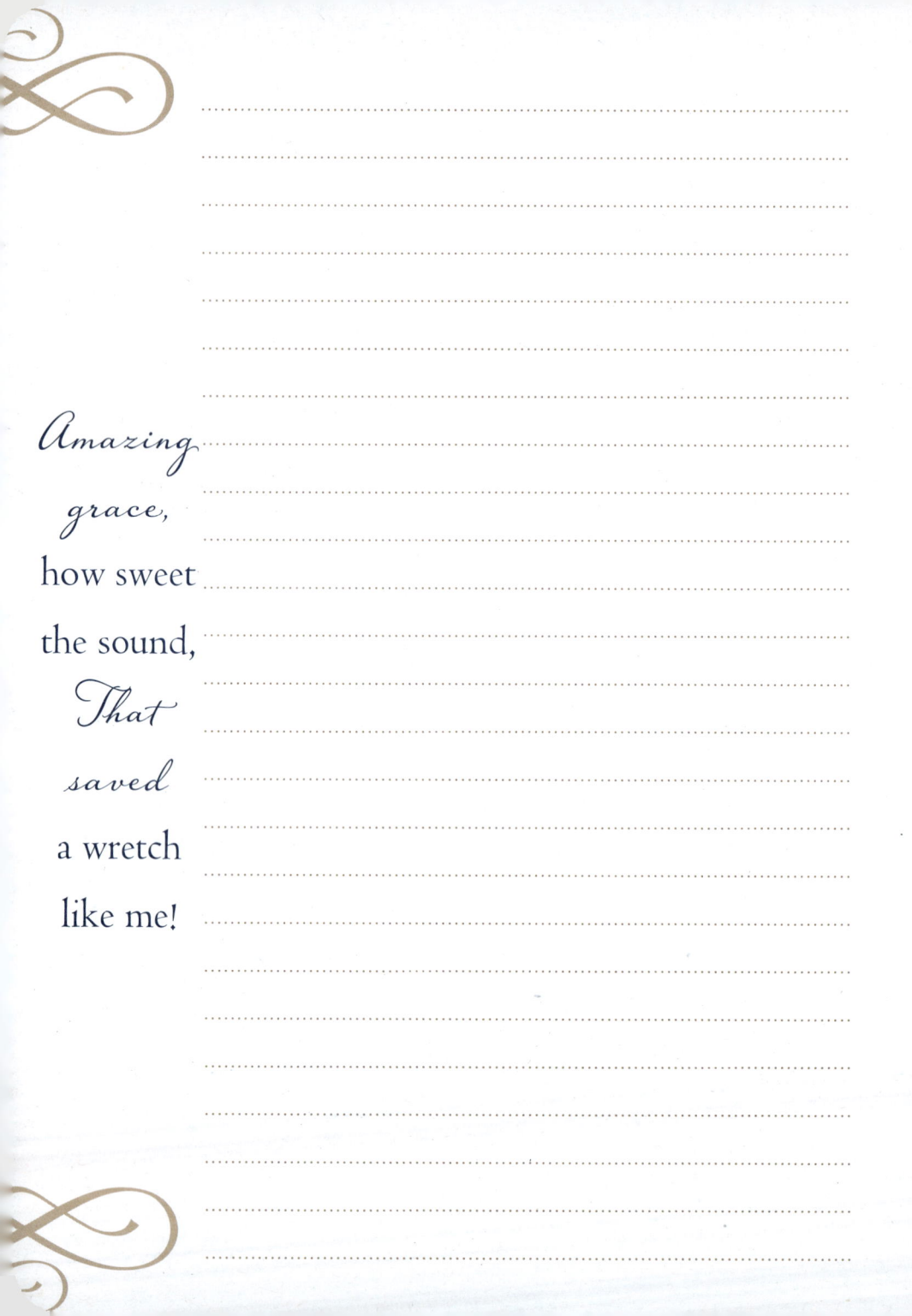

Amazing grace, how sweet the sound, That saved a wretch like me!

I once *was lost* but now am found, *Was blind* but now I see.

'Twas grace that taught my heart to fear, And grace my fears relieved;

How *precious* did that *grace* appear
The hour *I first believed!*

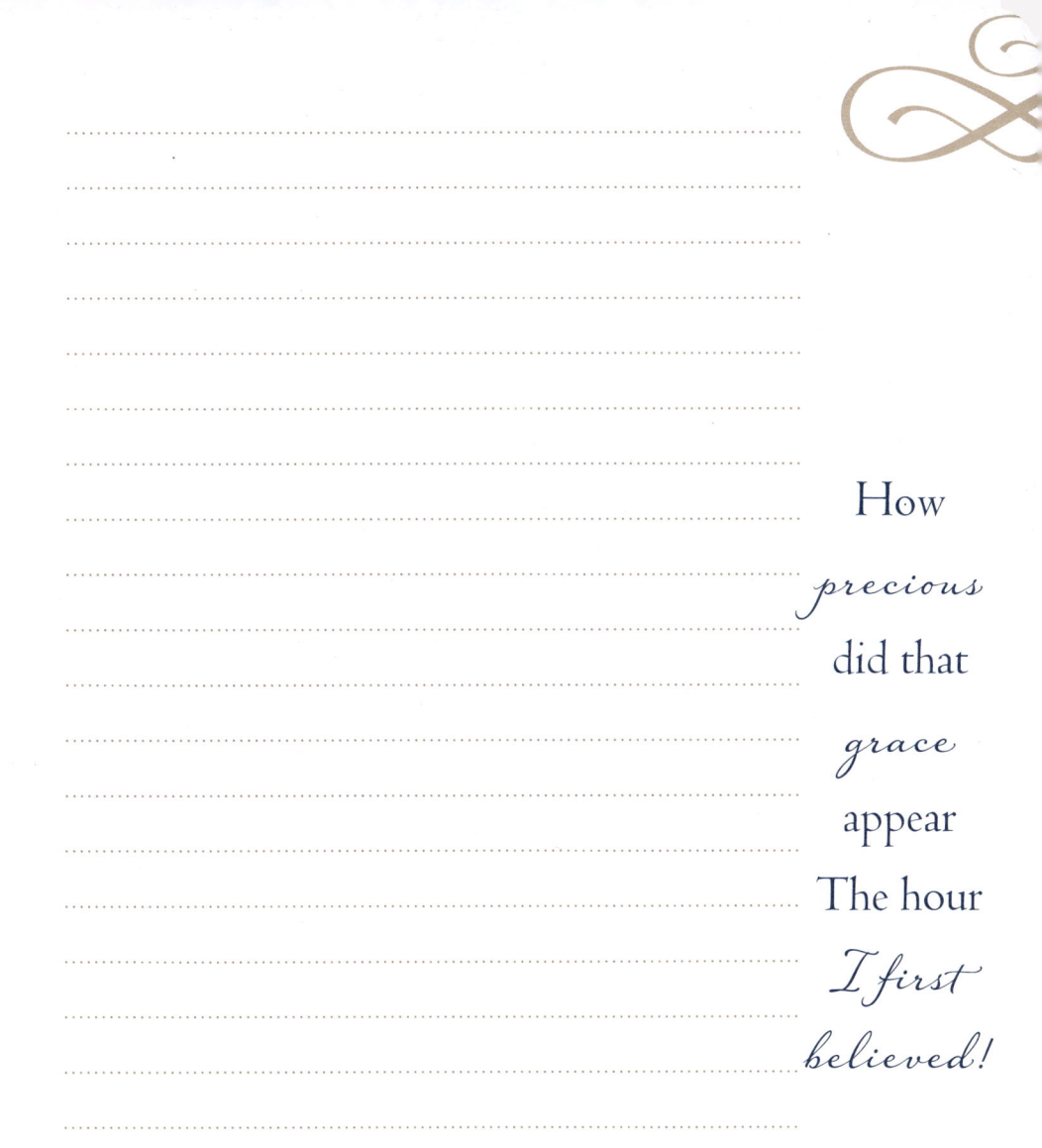

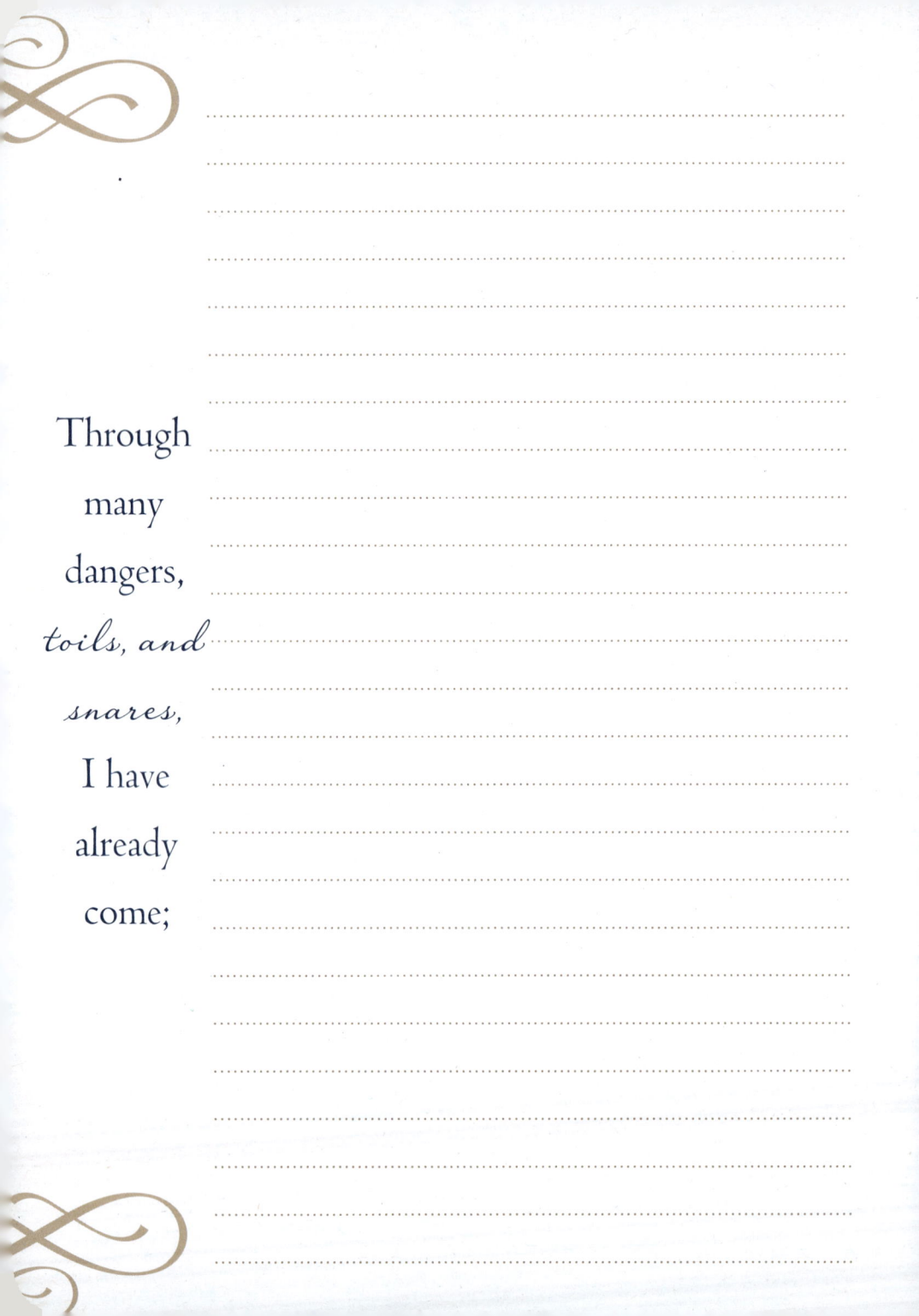

Through many dangers, toils, and snares, I have already come;

'Twas *grace* that brought me safe thus far, *And grace* will lead me home.

The Lord has promised good to me. His Word my hope secures.

He will my shield and portion be, As long as life endures.

The earth shall soon dissolve like snow, The sun forbear to shine;

*But God,
who called
me here
below,
Will be
forever
mine.*

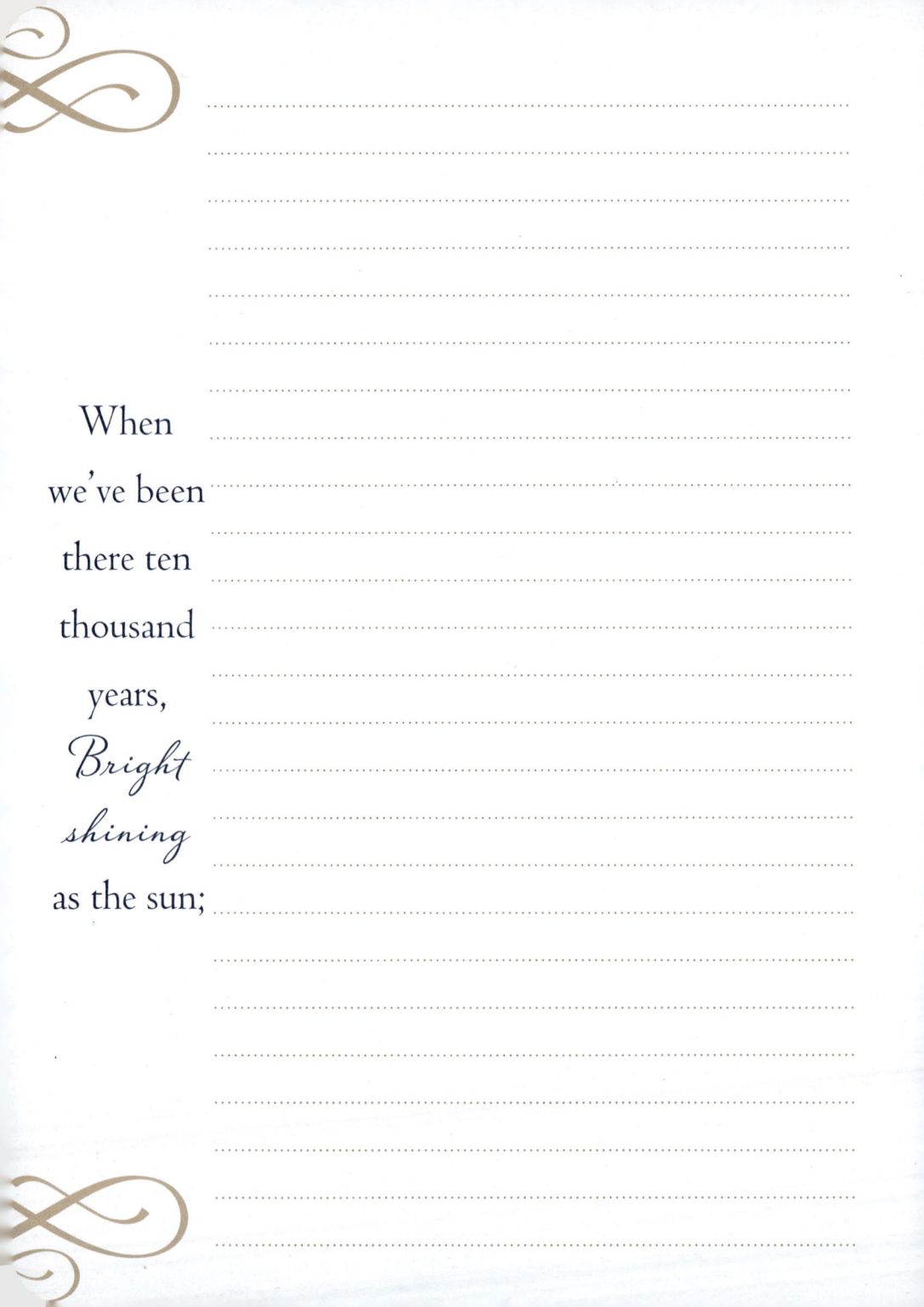

When we've been there ten thousand years, *Bright shining* as the sun;

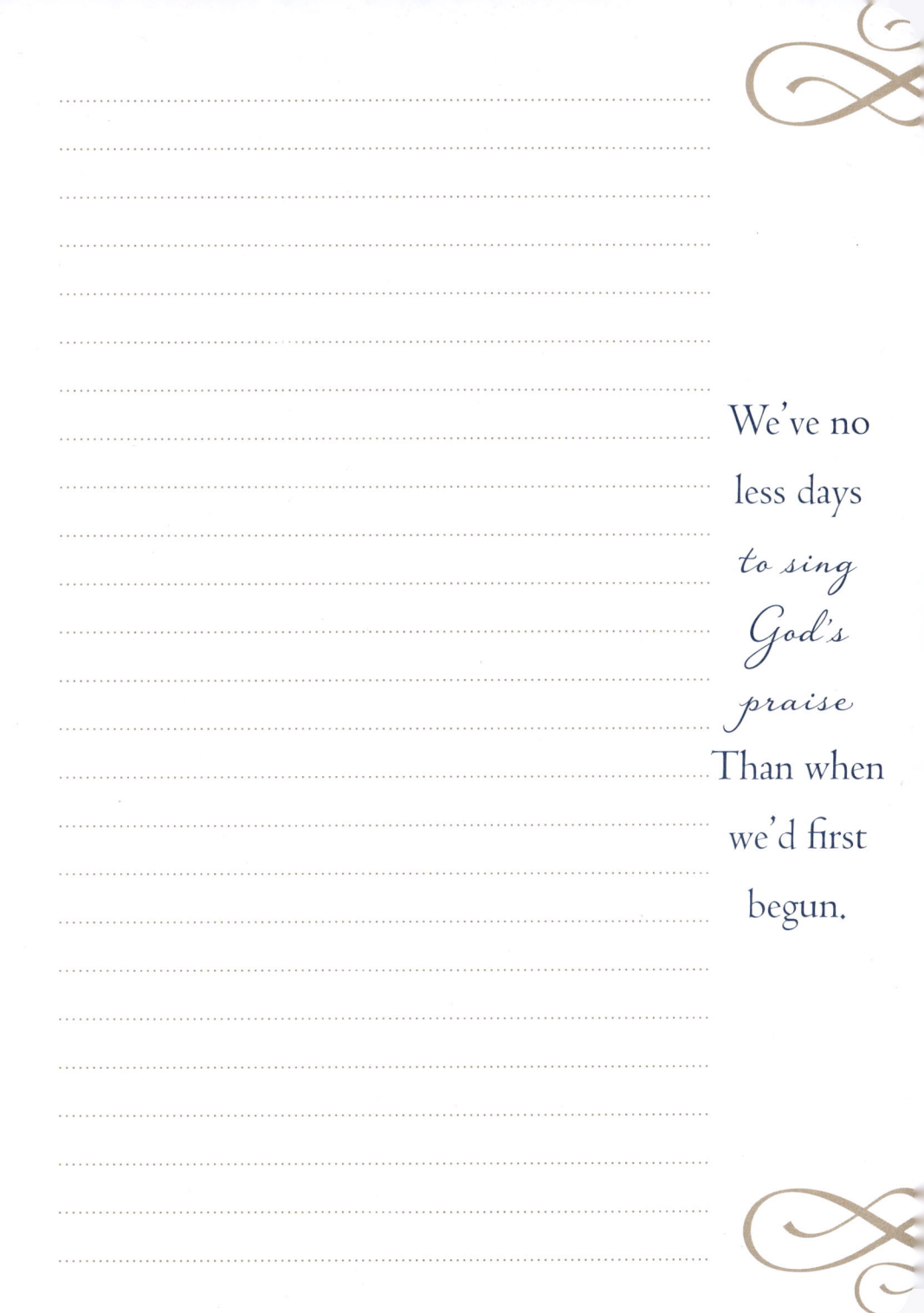

We've no less days *to sing God's praise* Than when we'd first begun.

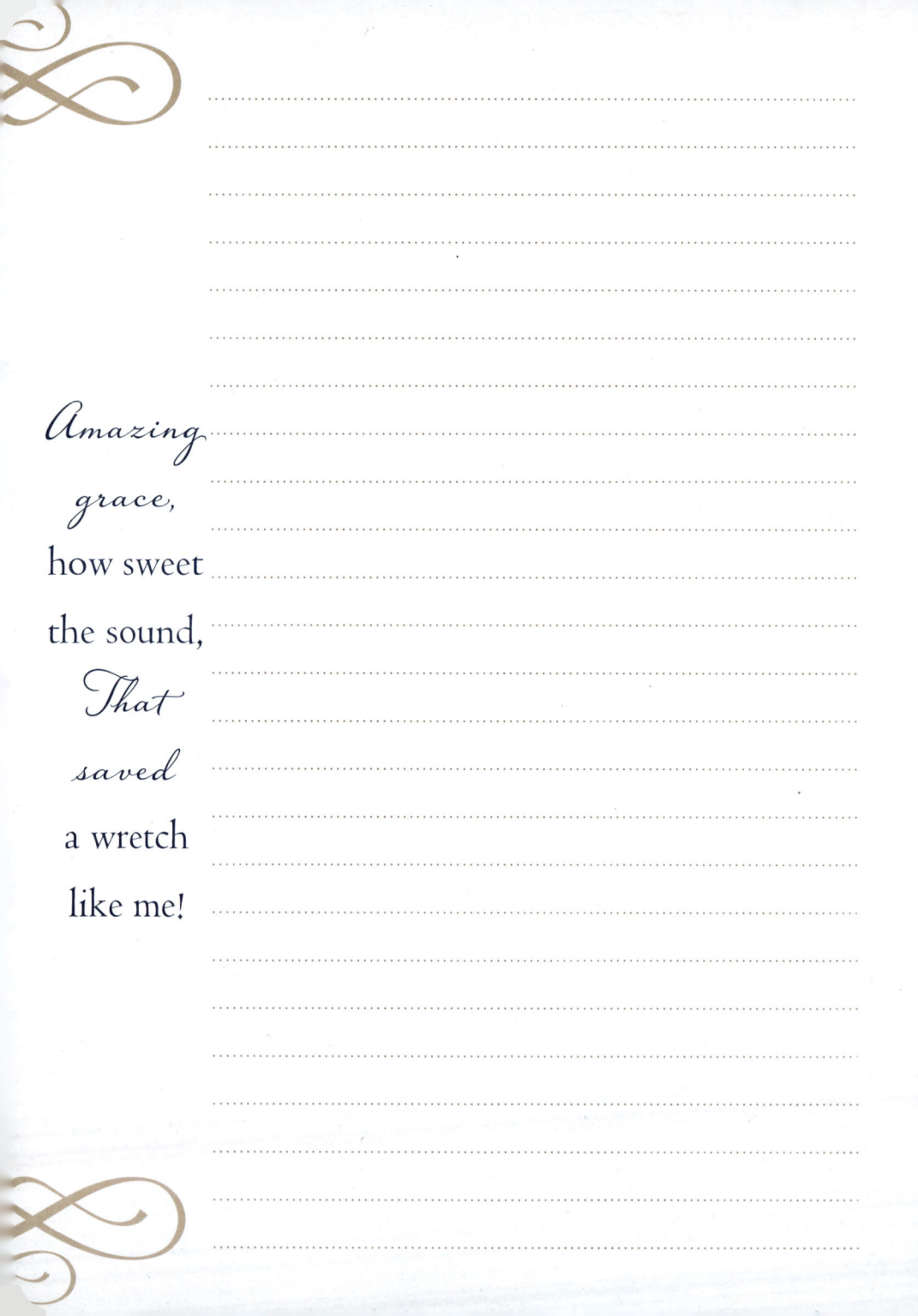

Amazing grace, how sweet the sound, That saved a wretch like me!

I once was lost but now am found, Was blind but now I see.

'Twas grace that taught my heart to fear, And grace my fears relieved;

How *precious* did that *grace* appear
The hour *I first believed!*

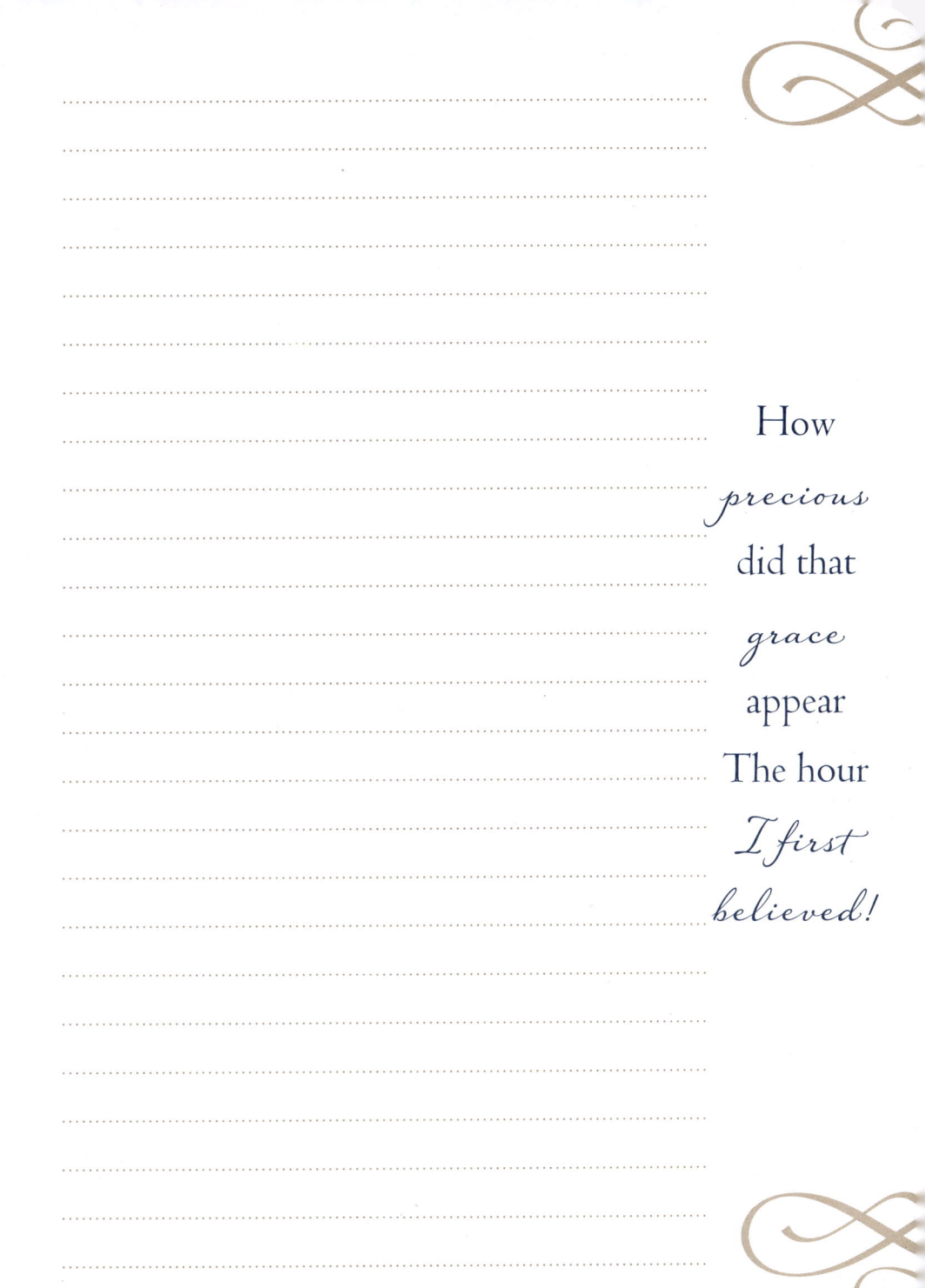

Through many dangers, toils, and snares, I have already come;

'Twas grace that brought me safe thus far, And grace will lead me home.

The Lord has promised good to me. His Word my hope secures.

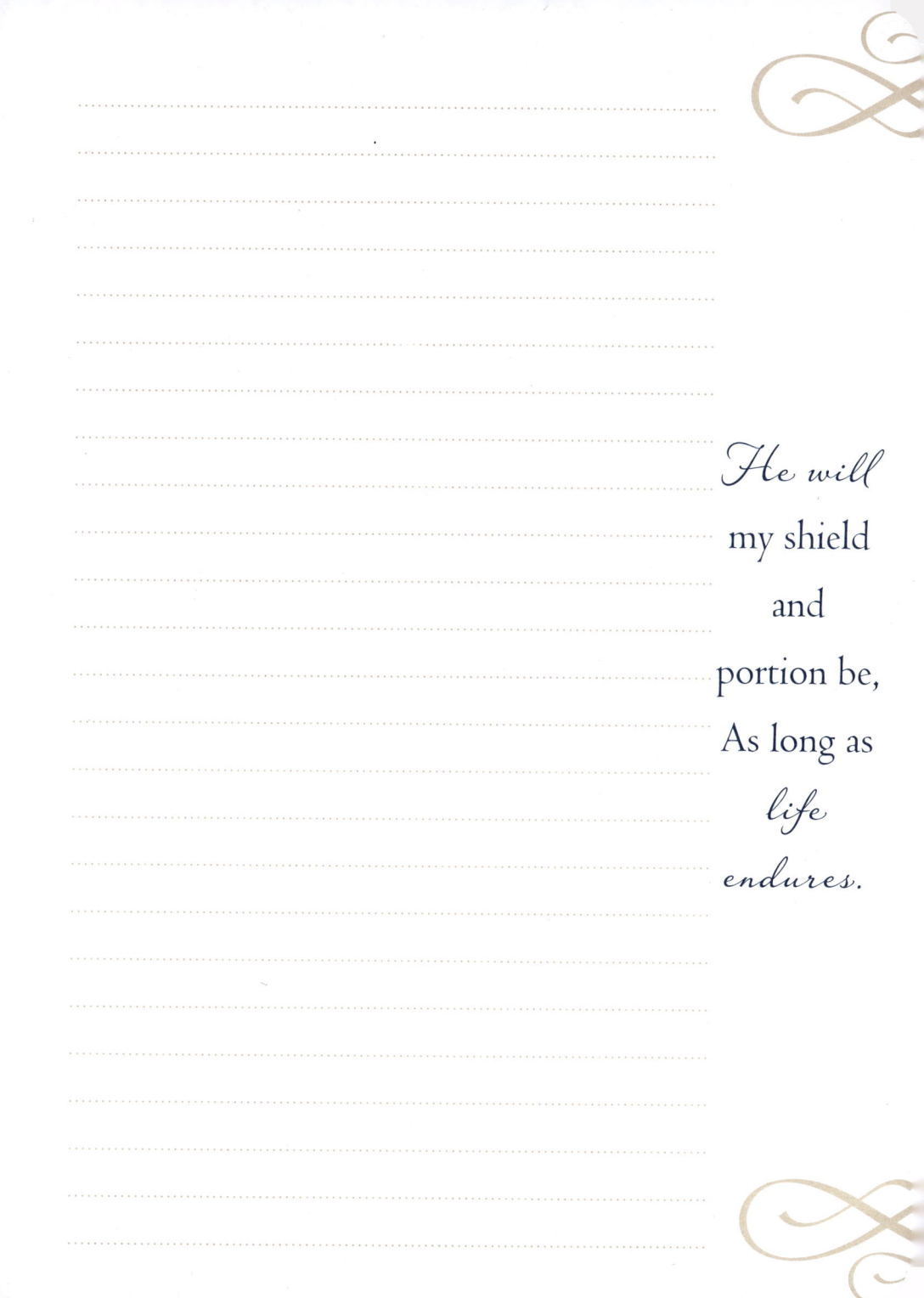

He will my shield and portion be, As long as life endures.

The earth shall soon dissolve like snow, The sun forbear to shine;

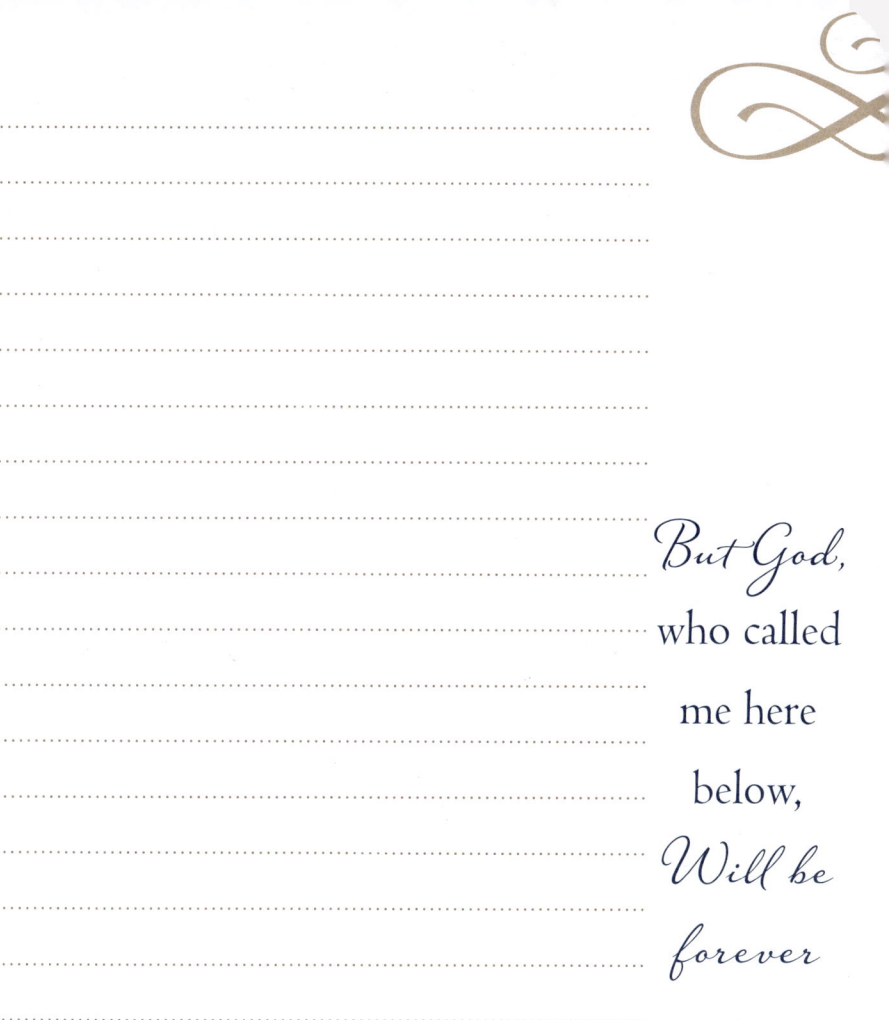

But God, who called me here below, Will be forever mine.

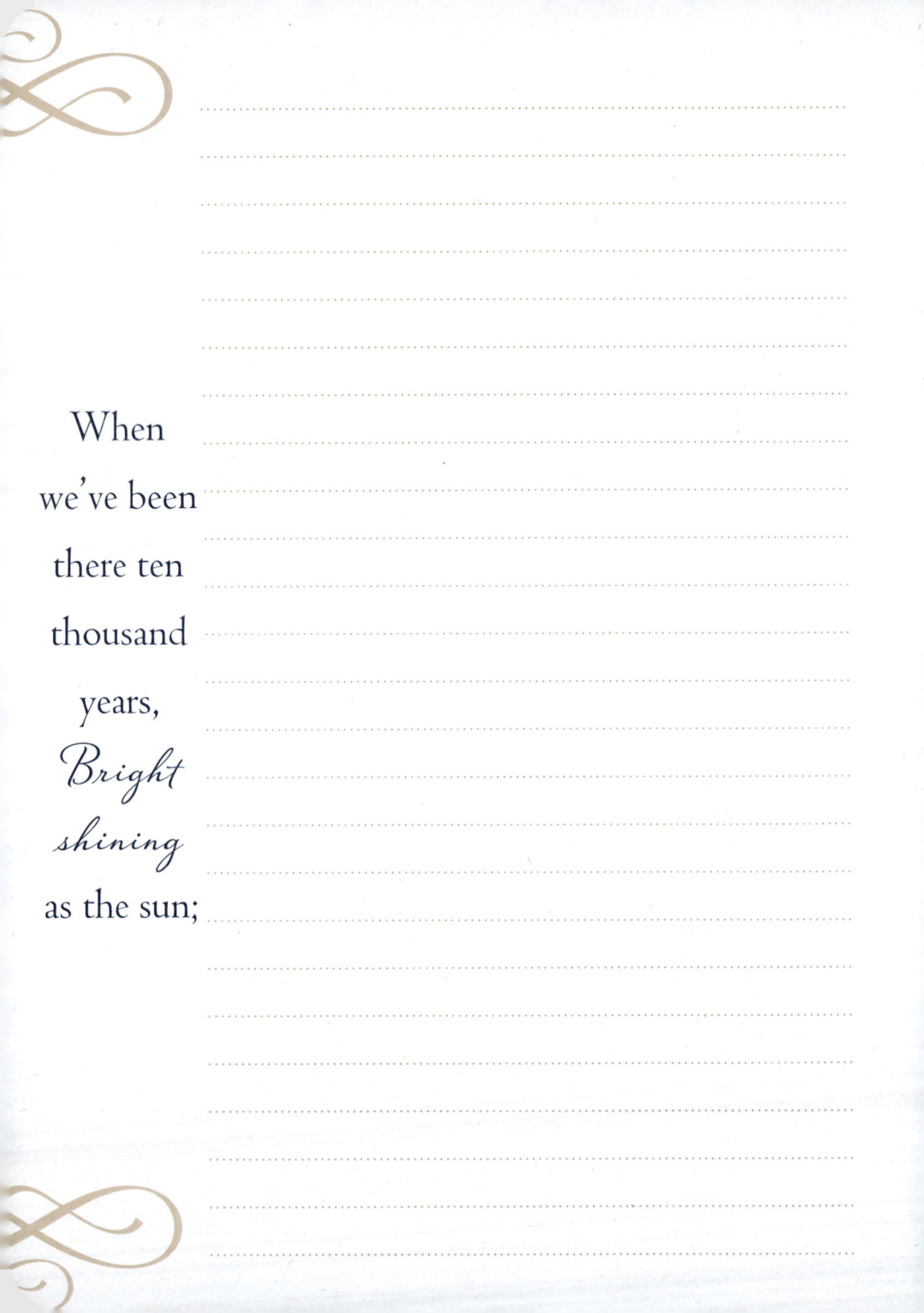

When we've been there ten thousand years,
Bright shining as the sun;

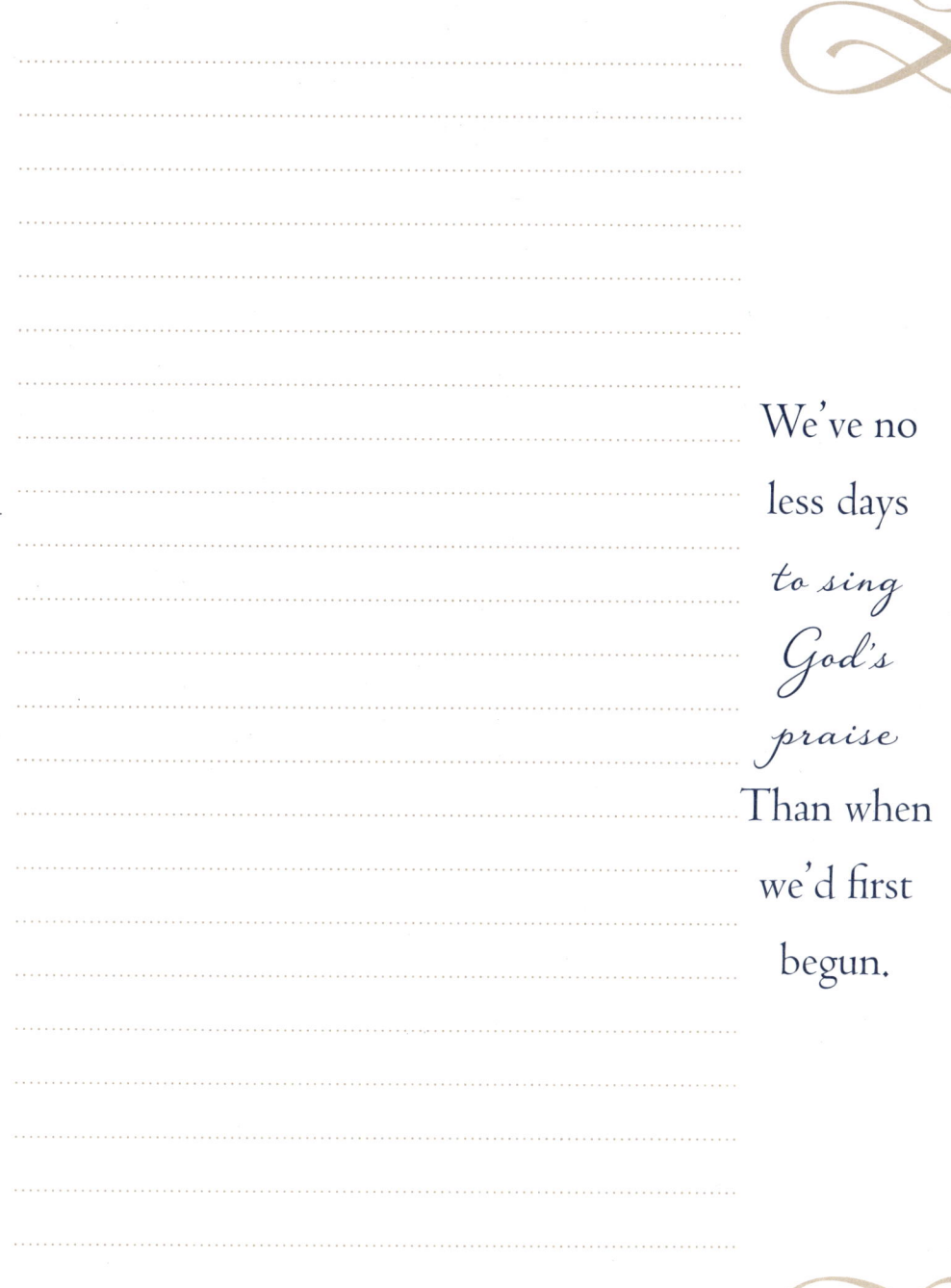

We've no less days *to sing God's praise* Than when we'd first begun.

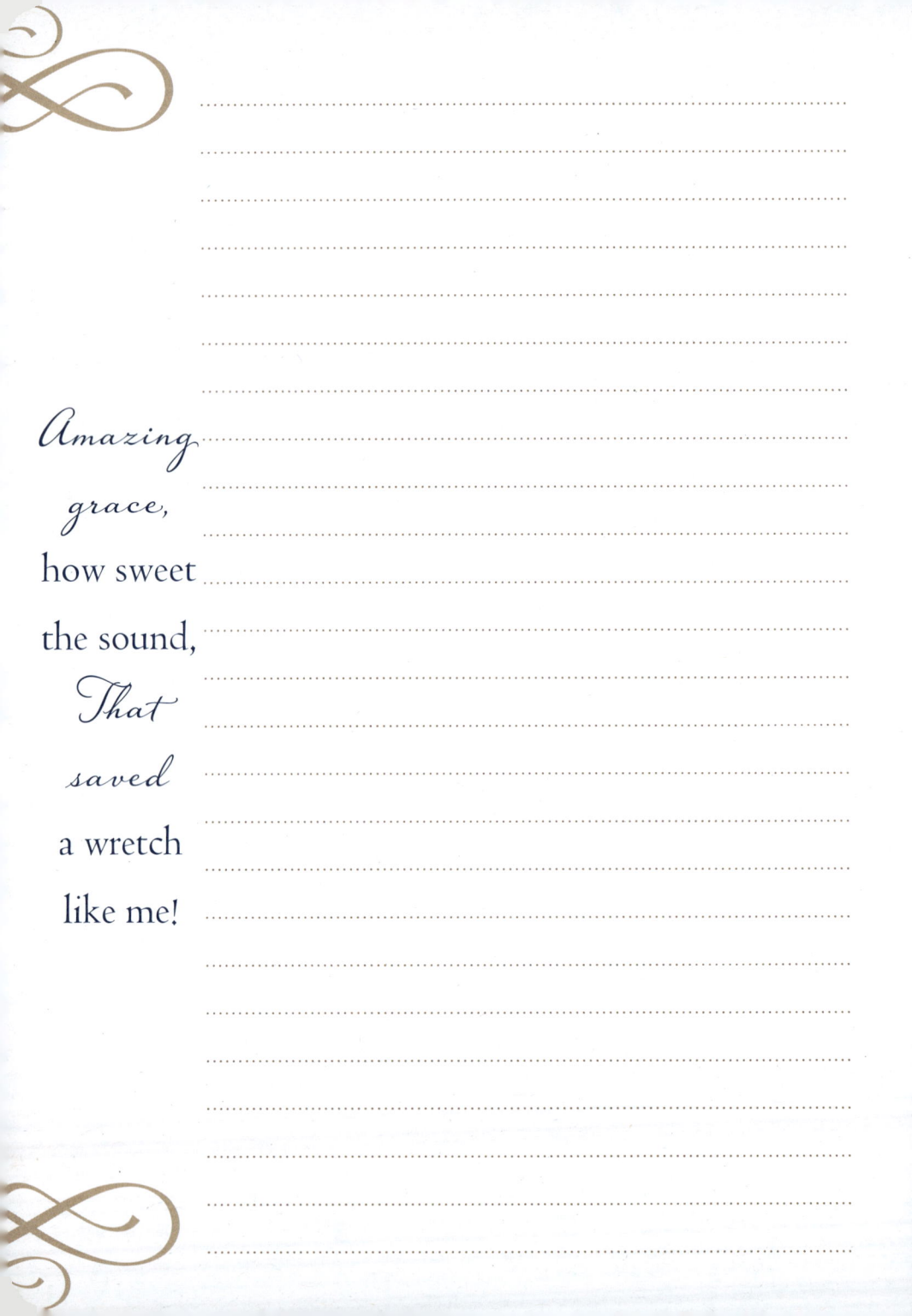

Amazing grace, how sweet the sound, That saved a wretch like me!

I once *was lost* but now am found, *Was blind* but now I see.

'Twas grace that taught my heart to fear, And grace my fears relieved;

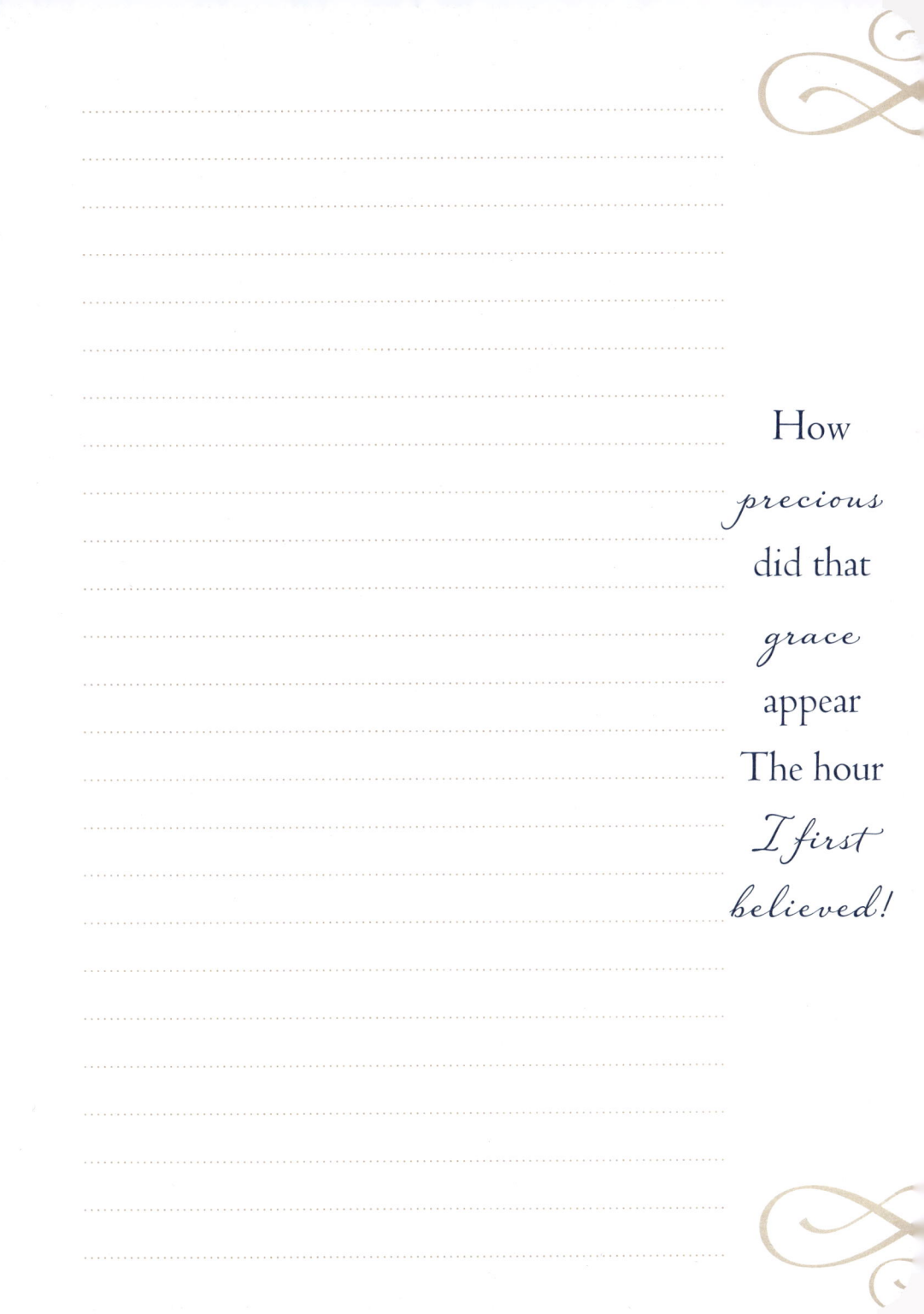

How *precious* did that *grace* appear
The hour *I first believed!*

> Through many dangers, toils, and snares, I have already come;

'Twas *grace* that brought me safe thus far, *And grace* will lead me home.

The Lord has promised good to me. His Word my hope secures.

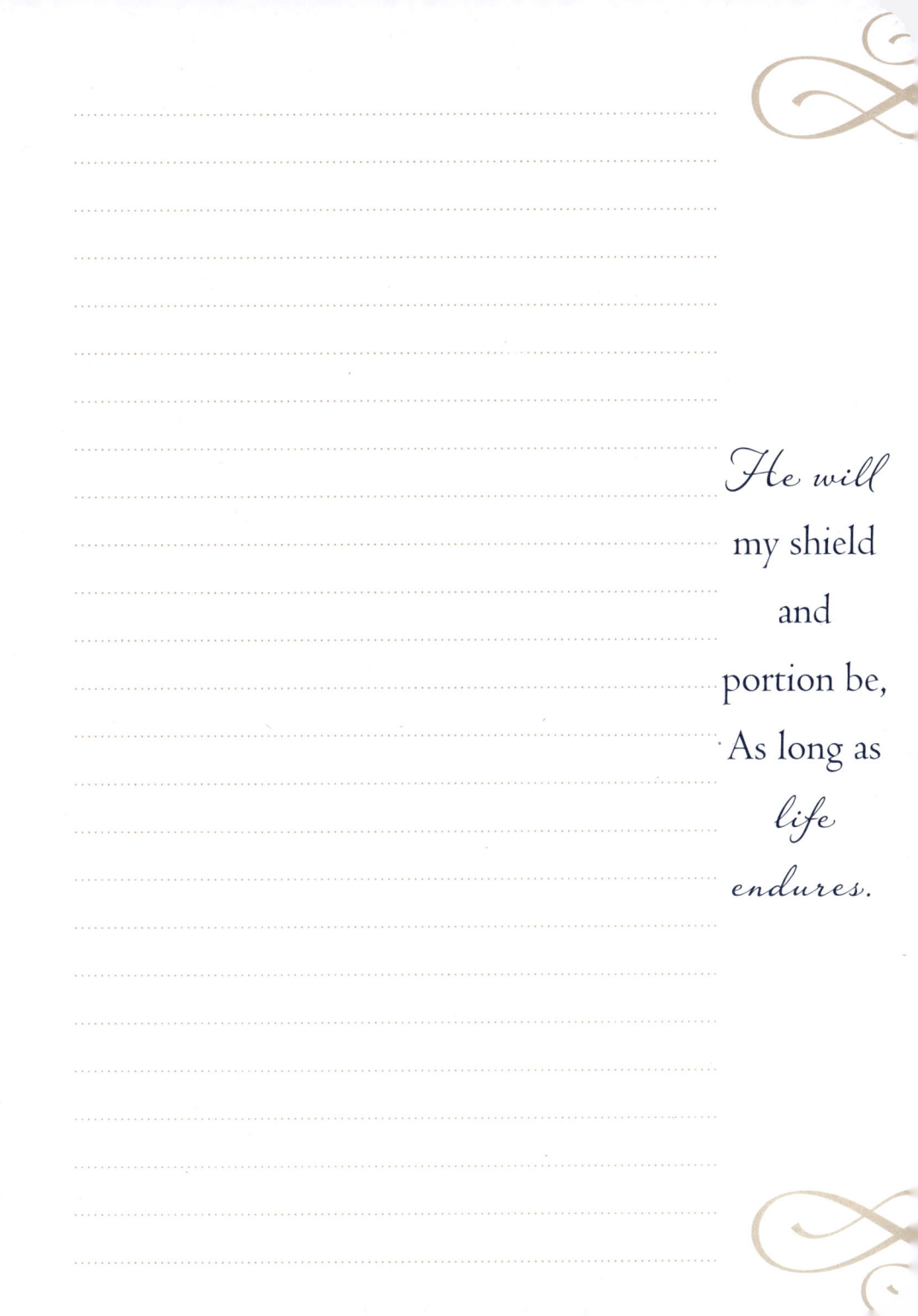

He will my shield and portion be, As long as life endures.

The earth shall soon dissolve like snow, The sun forbear to shine;

But God, who called me here below, Will be forever mine.

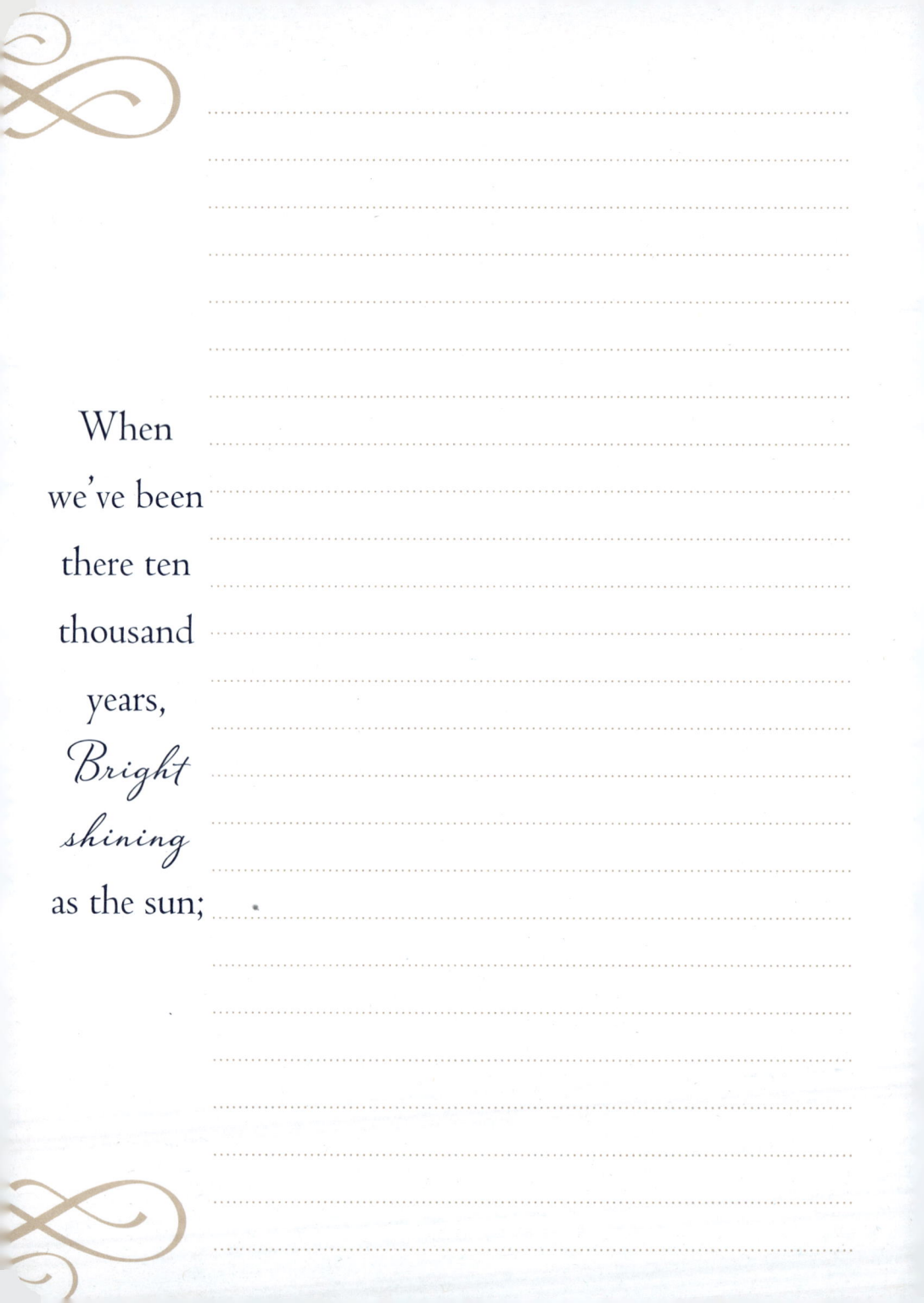

When
we've been
there ten
thousand
years,
*Bright
shining
as the sun;*

We've no less days *to sing God's praise* Than when we'd first begun.

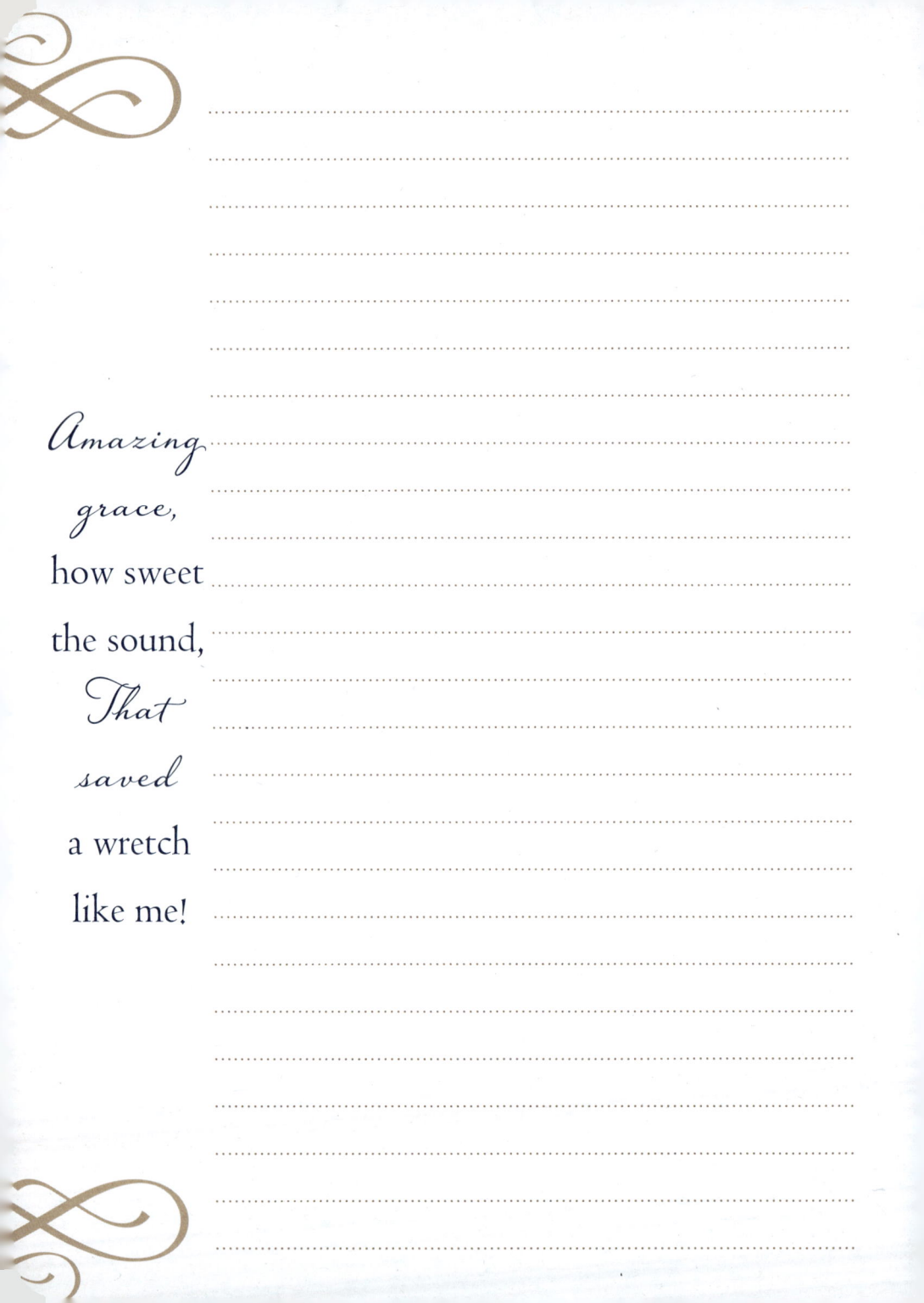

Amazing grace, how sweet the sound, That saved a wretch like me!

I once *was lost* but now am found, *Was blind* but now I see.

'Twas grace that taught my heart to fear, And grace my fears relieved;

How *precious* did that *grace* appear The hour *I first believed!*

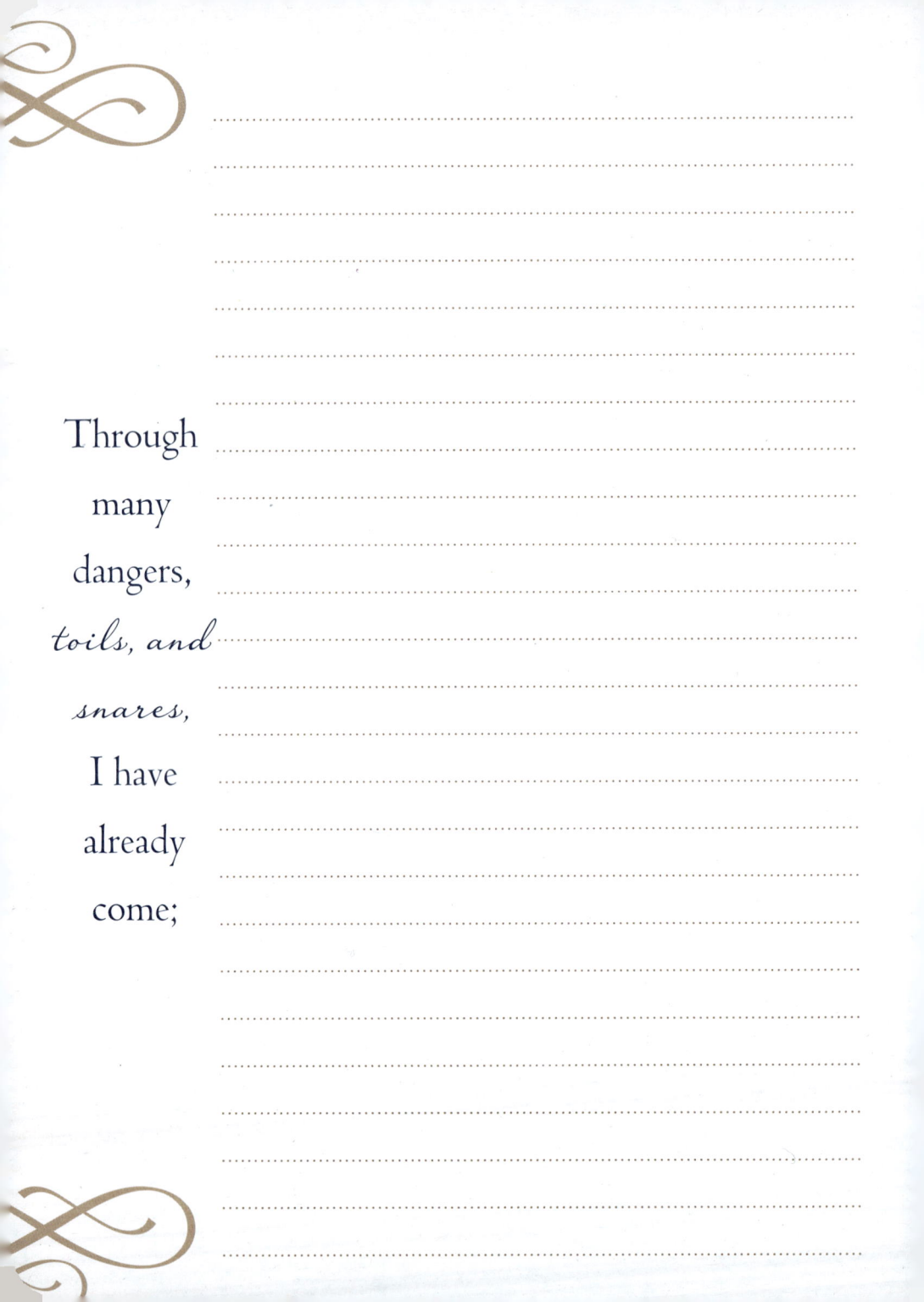

Through many dangers, toils, and snares, I have already come;

'Twas *grace* that brought me safe thus far, *And grace* will lead me home.

The Lord has promised good to me. His Word my hope secures.

He will my shield and portion be, As long as life endures.

The earth
shall soon
dissolve
like snow,
The sun
forbear
to shine;

But God, who called me here below, Will be forever mine.

When
we've been
there ten
thousand
years,
*Bright
shining*
as the sun;

We've no less days to sing God's praise Than when we'd first begun.

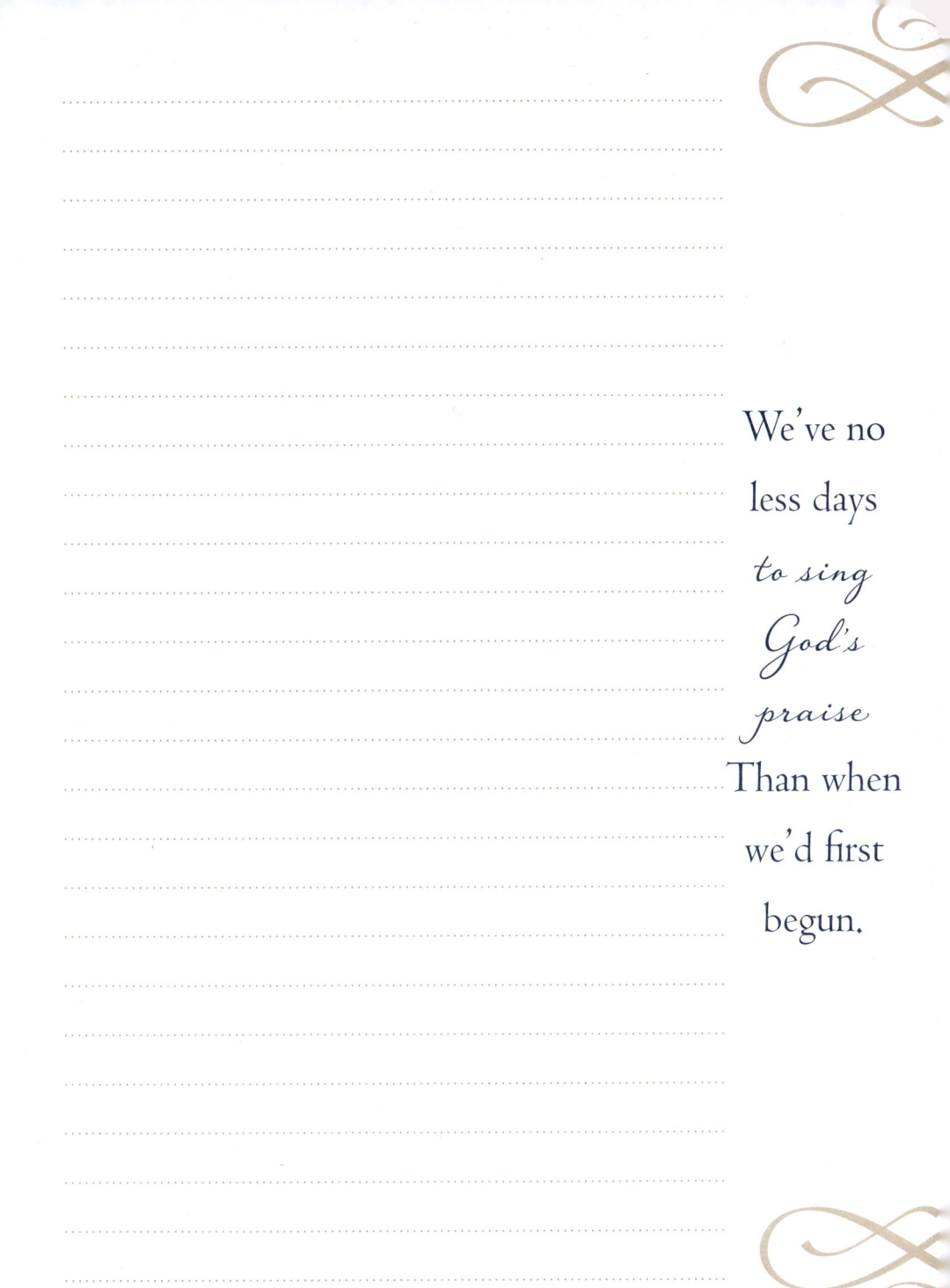

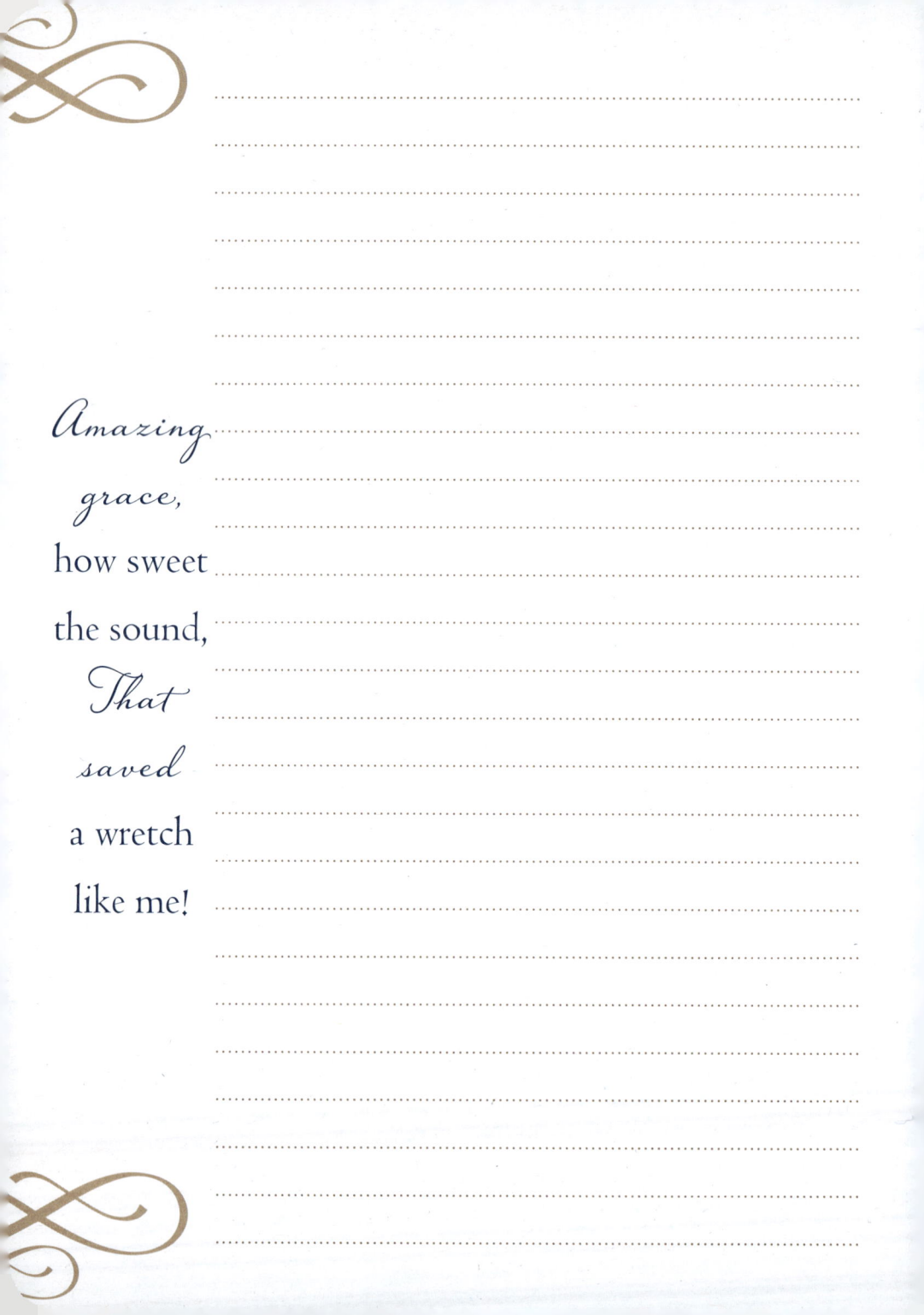

Amazing grace, how sweet the sound, That saved a wretch like me!

I once *was lost* but now am found, *Was blind* but now I see.

'Twas grace that taught my heart to fear, And grace my fears relieved;

How *precious* did that *grace* appear
The hour *I first believed!*

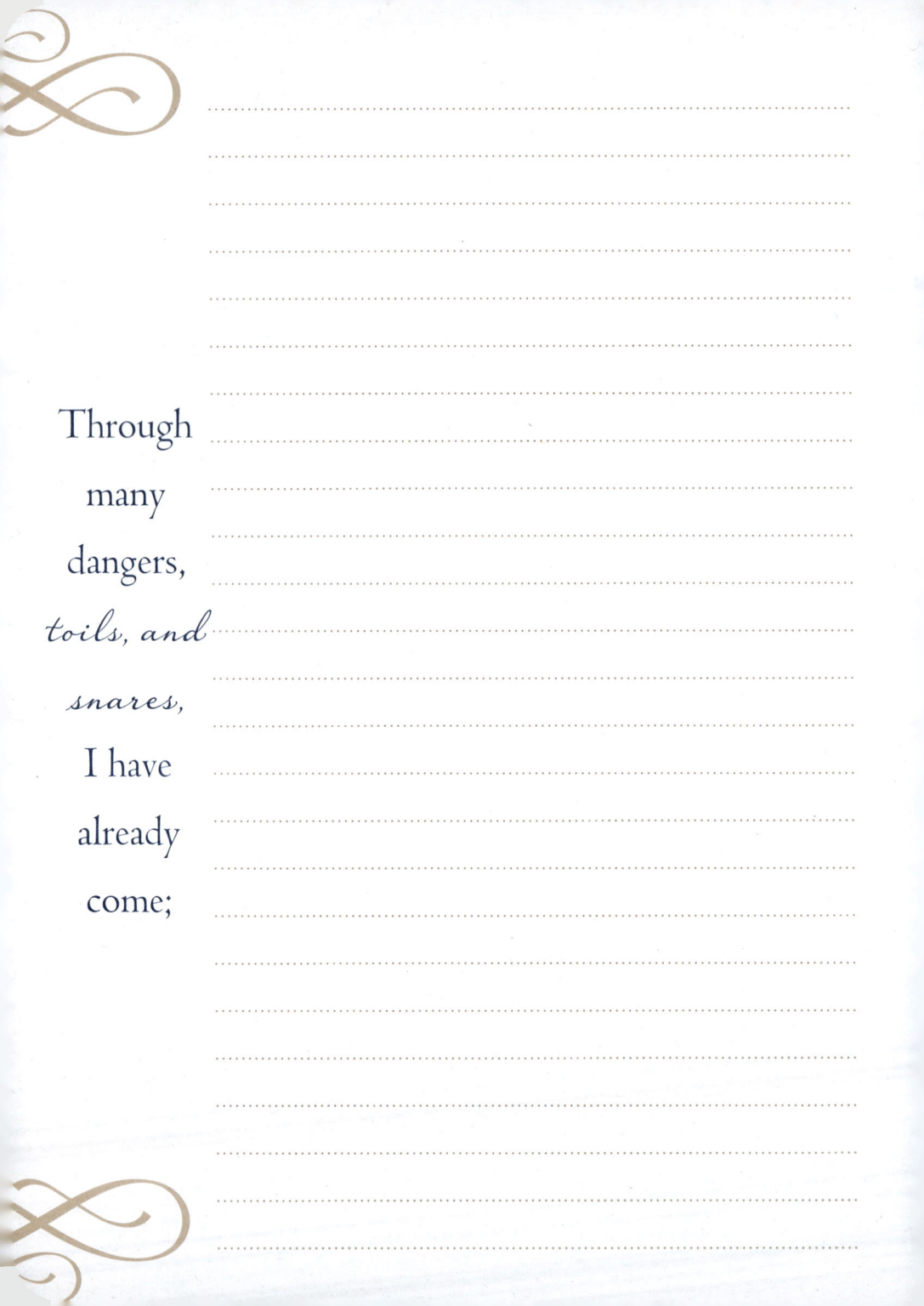

> Through many dangers, toils, and snares, I have already come;

'Twas *grace* that brought me safe thus far, *And* *grace* will lead me home.

The Lord has promised good to me. His Word my hope secures.

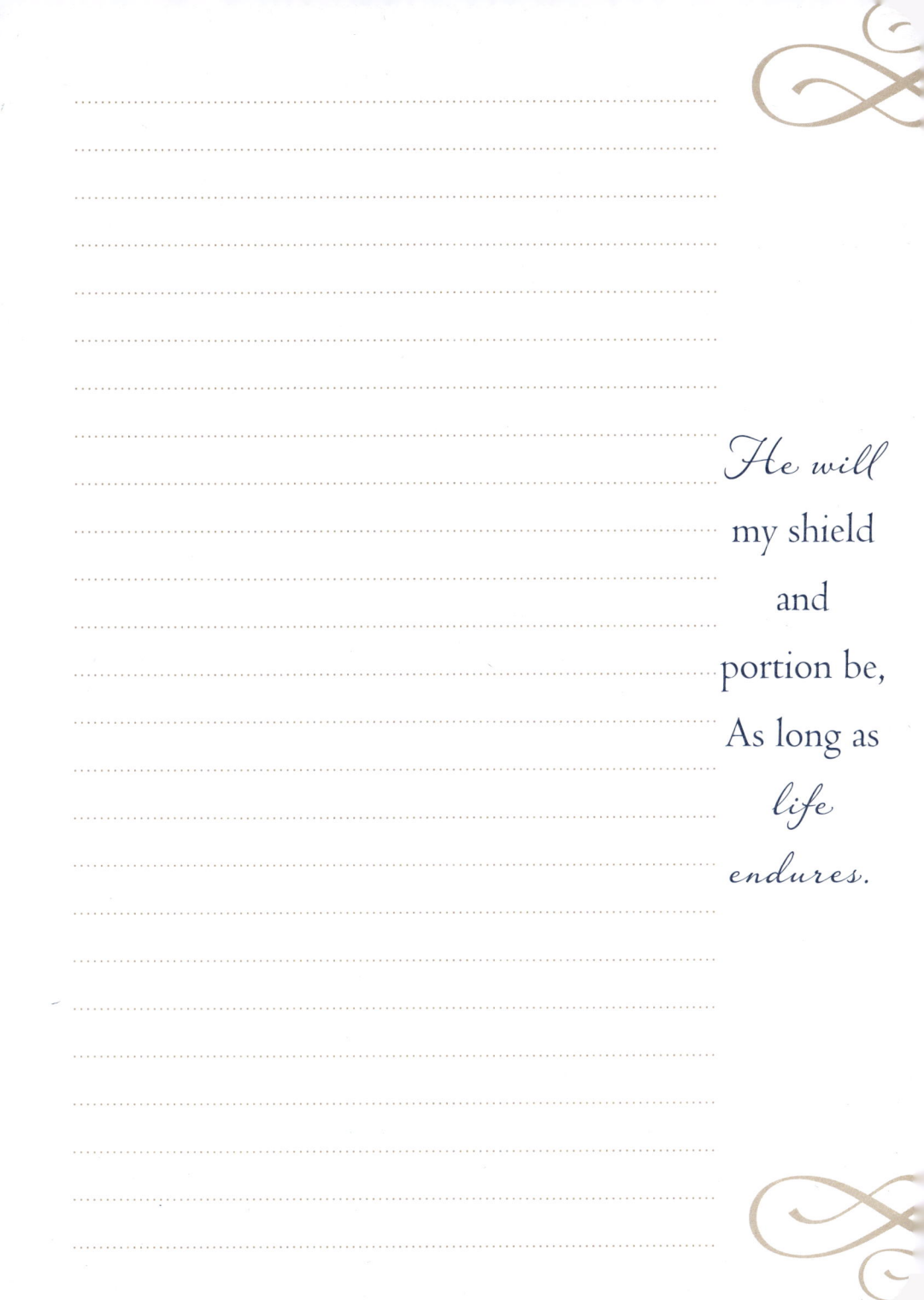

He will my shield and portion be, As long as life endures.

The earth shall soon dissolve like snow, The sun forbear to shine;

*But God,
who called
me here
below,
Will be
forever
mine.*

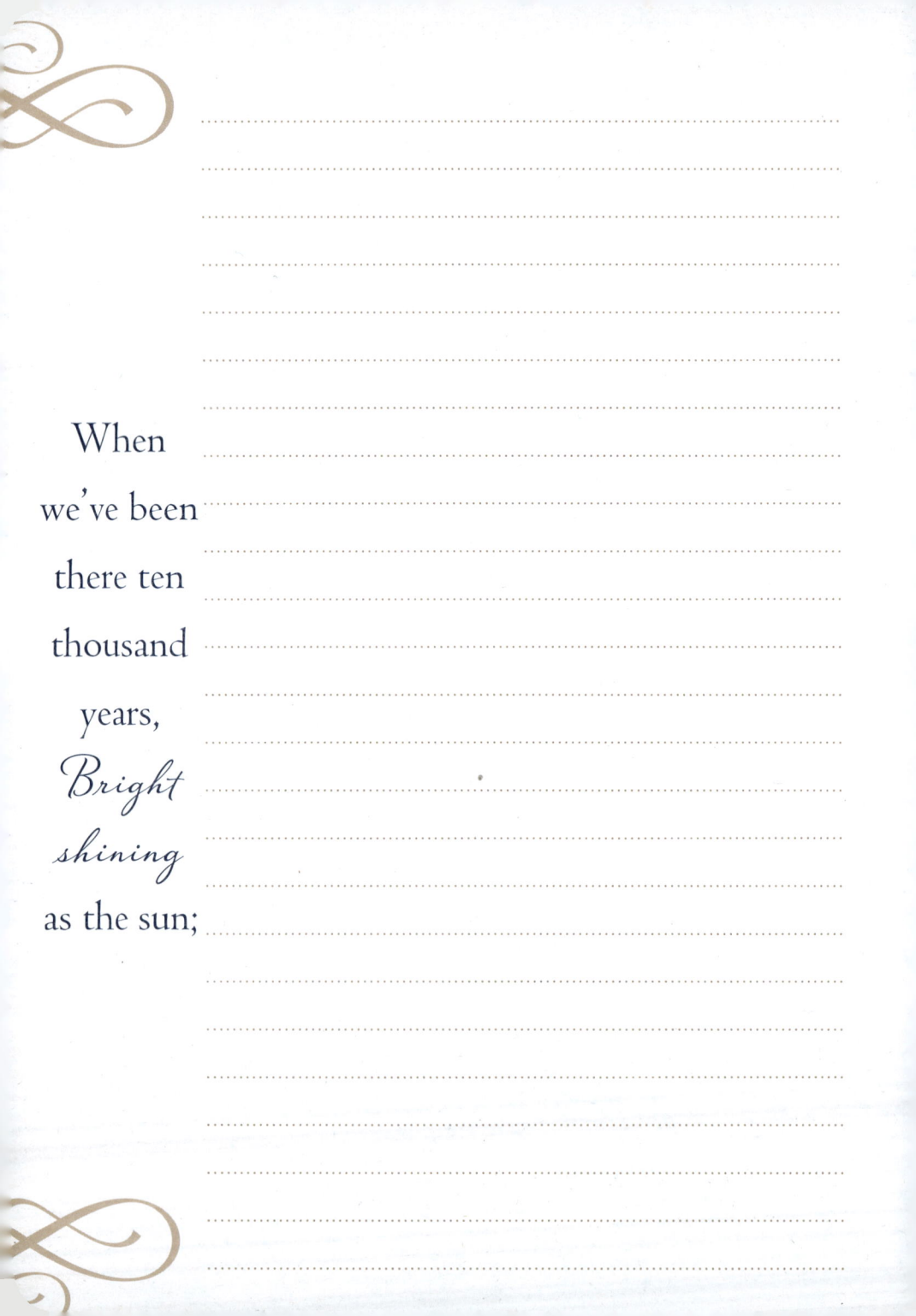

When we've been there ten thousand years,
Bright shining as the sun;

We've no less days *to sing God's praise* Than when we'd first begun.

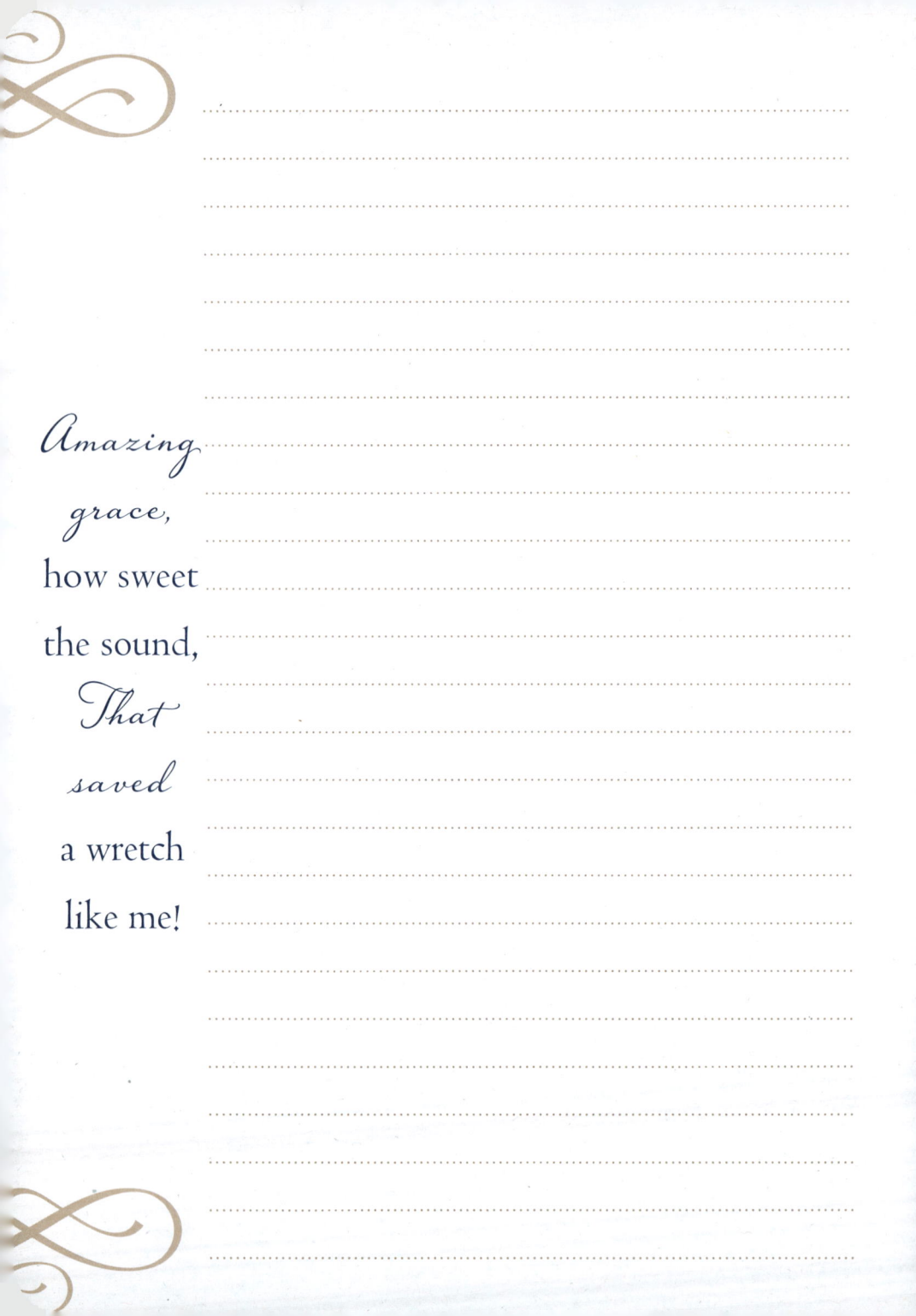

Amazing grace, how sweet the sound, That saved a wretch like me!

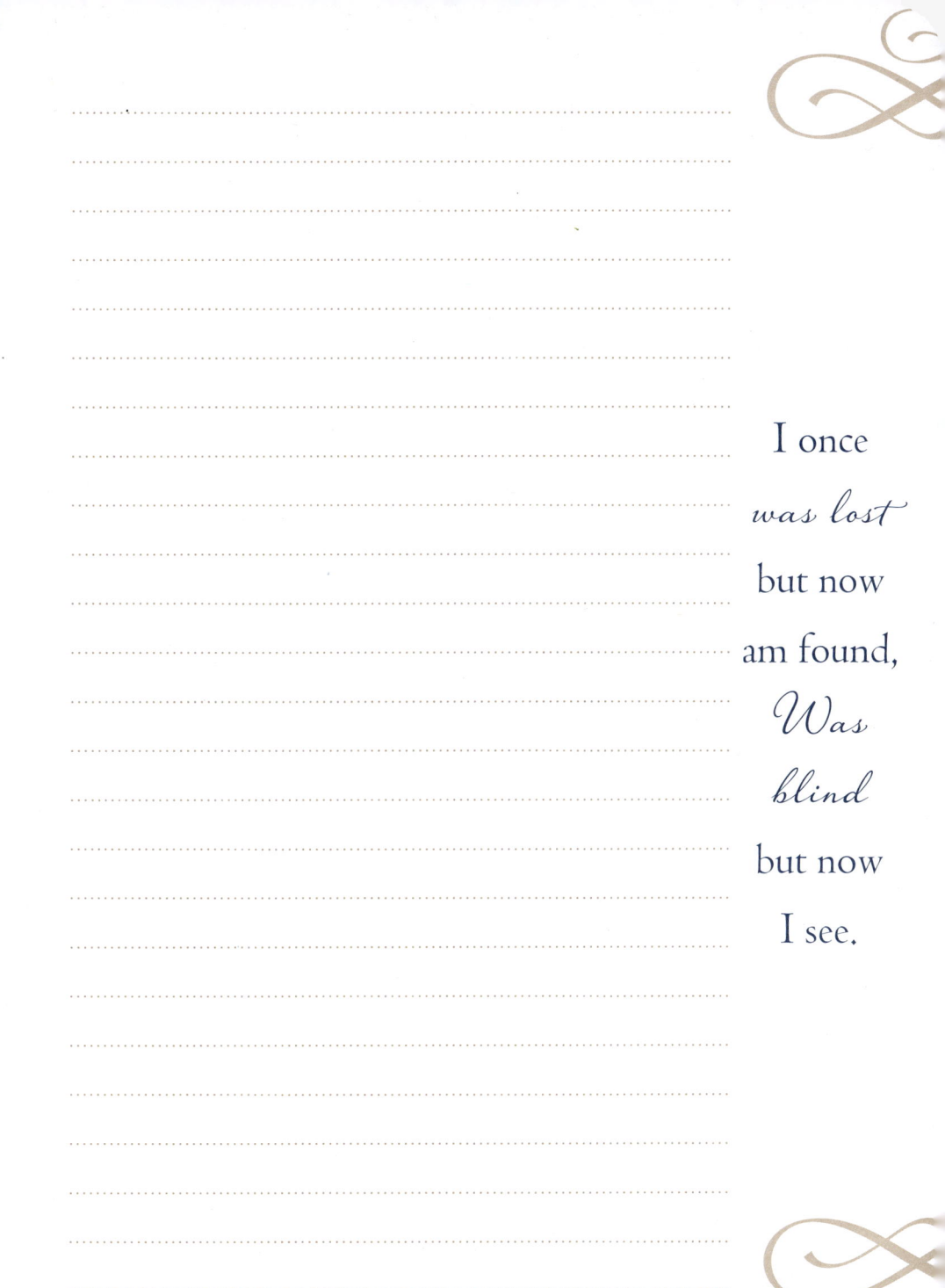

I once was lost but now am found, *Was blind* but now I see.

'Twas grace that taught my heart to fear, And grace my fears relieved;

How *precious* did that *grace* appear
The hour *I first believed!*

Through many dangers, toils, and snares, I have already come;

'Twas grace that brought me safe thus far, And grace will lead me home.

The Lord has promised good to me. His Word my hope secures.

He will my shield and portion be, As long as life endures.

The earth shall soon dissolve like snow, The sun forbear to shine;

> But God, who called me here below, Will be forever mine.

When
we've been
there ten
thousand
years,
*Bright
shining
as the sun;*

> We've no less days *to sing God's praise* Than when we'd first begun.

Amazing grace, how sweet the sound, That saved a wretch like me!

I once *was lost* but now am found, *Was blind* but now I see.

'Twas grace that taught my heart to fear,
And grace my fears relieved;

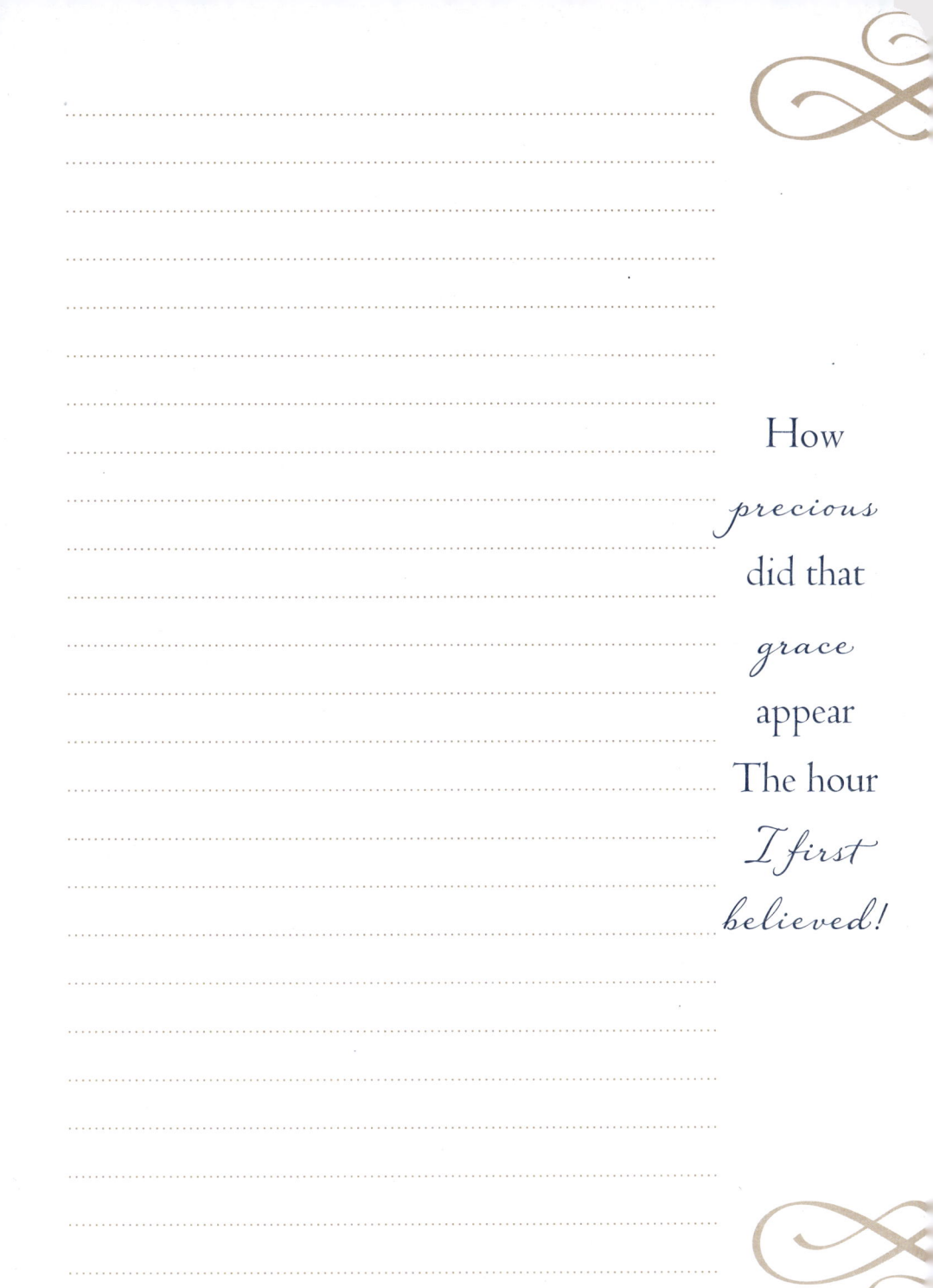

How precious did that grace appear The hour I first believed!

Through many dangers, toils, and snares, I have already come;

'Twas *grace* that brought me safe thus far, *And grace* will lead me home.

The Lord has promised good to me. His Word my hope secures.

He will my shield and portion be, As long as life endures.

The earth shall soon dissolve like snow, The sun forbear to shine;

But God, who called me here below, Will be forever mine.

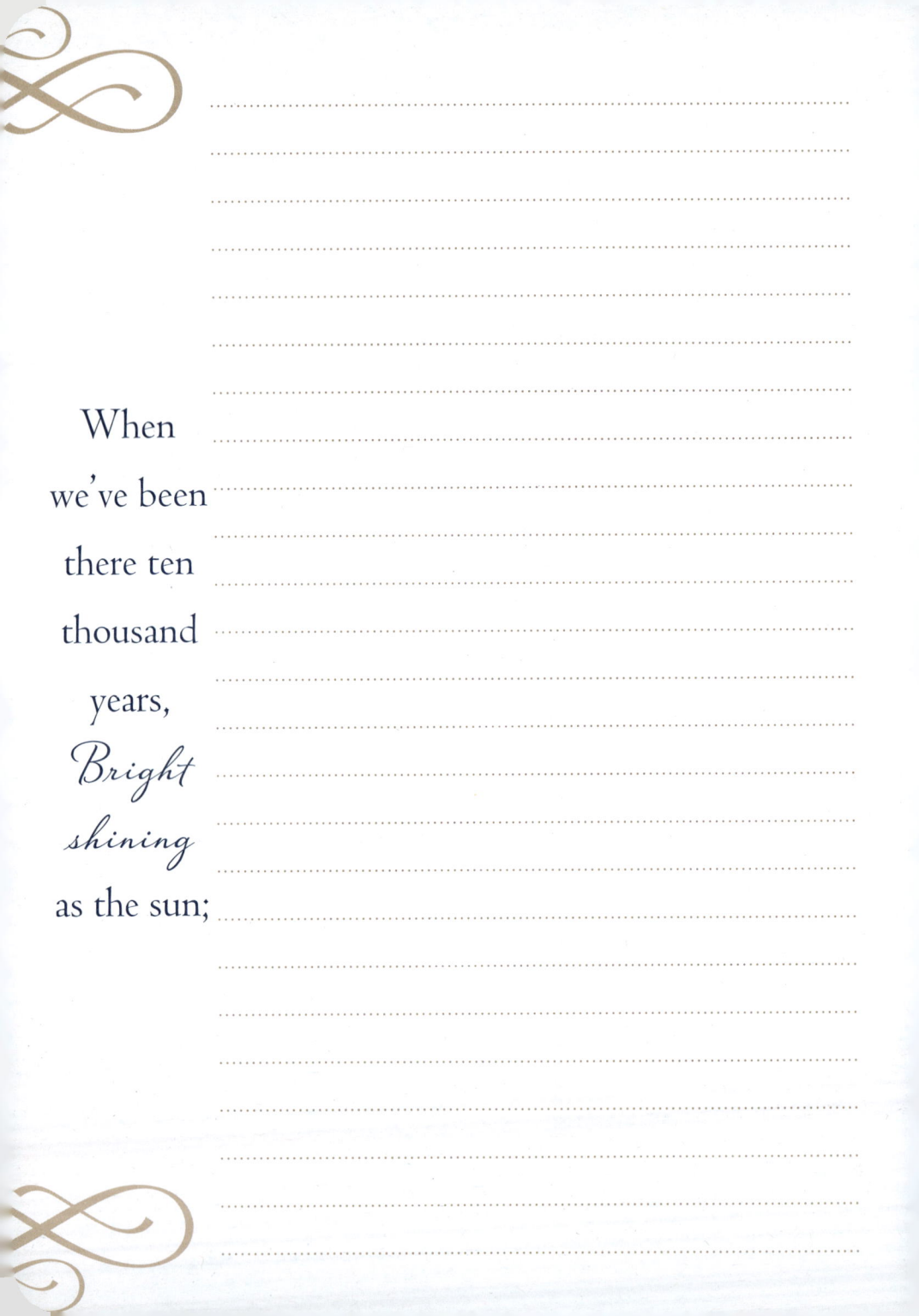

When
we've been
there ten
thousand
years,
*Bright
shining*
as the sun;

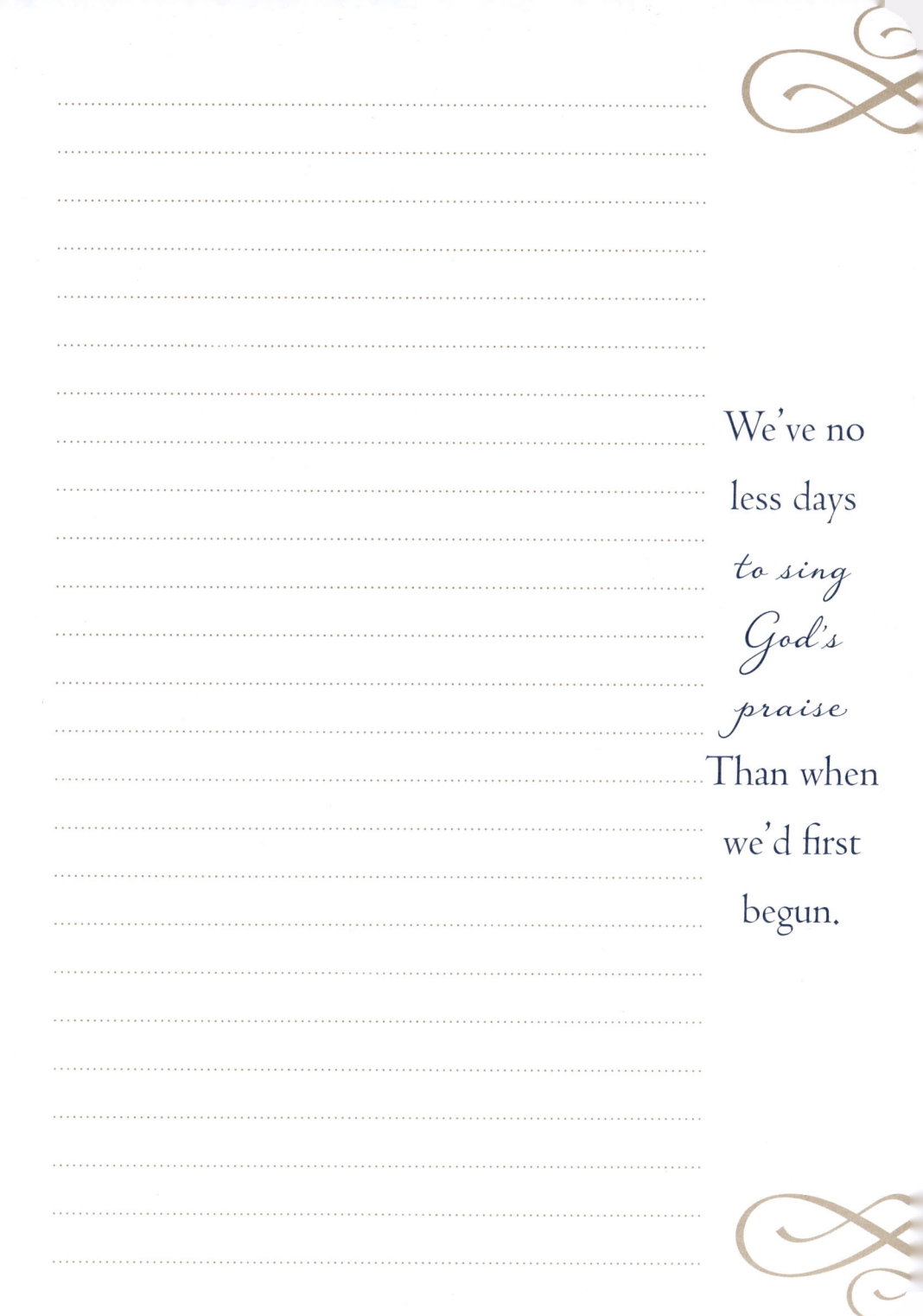

We've no less days *to sing God's praise* Than when we'd first begun.

Amazing grace, how sweet the sound, That saved a wretch like me!

I once
was lost
but now
am found,
Was
blind
but now
I see.

'Twas grace that taught my heart to fear, And grace my fears relieved;

How *precious* did that *grace* appear The hour *I first believed!*

Through many dangers, *toils, and snares,* I have already come;

'Twas *grace* that brought me safe thus far, *And grace* will lead me home.

The Lord has promised good to me. His Word my hope secures.

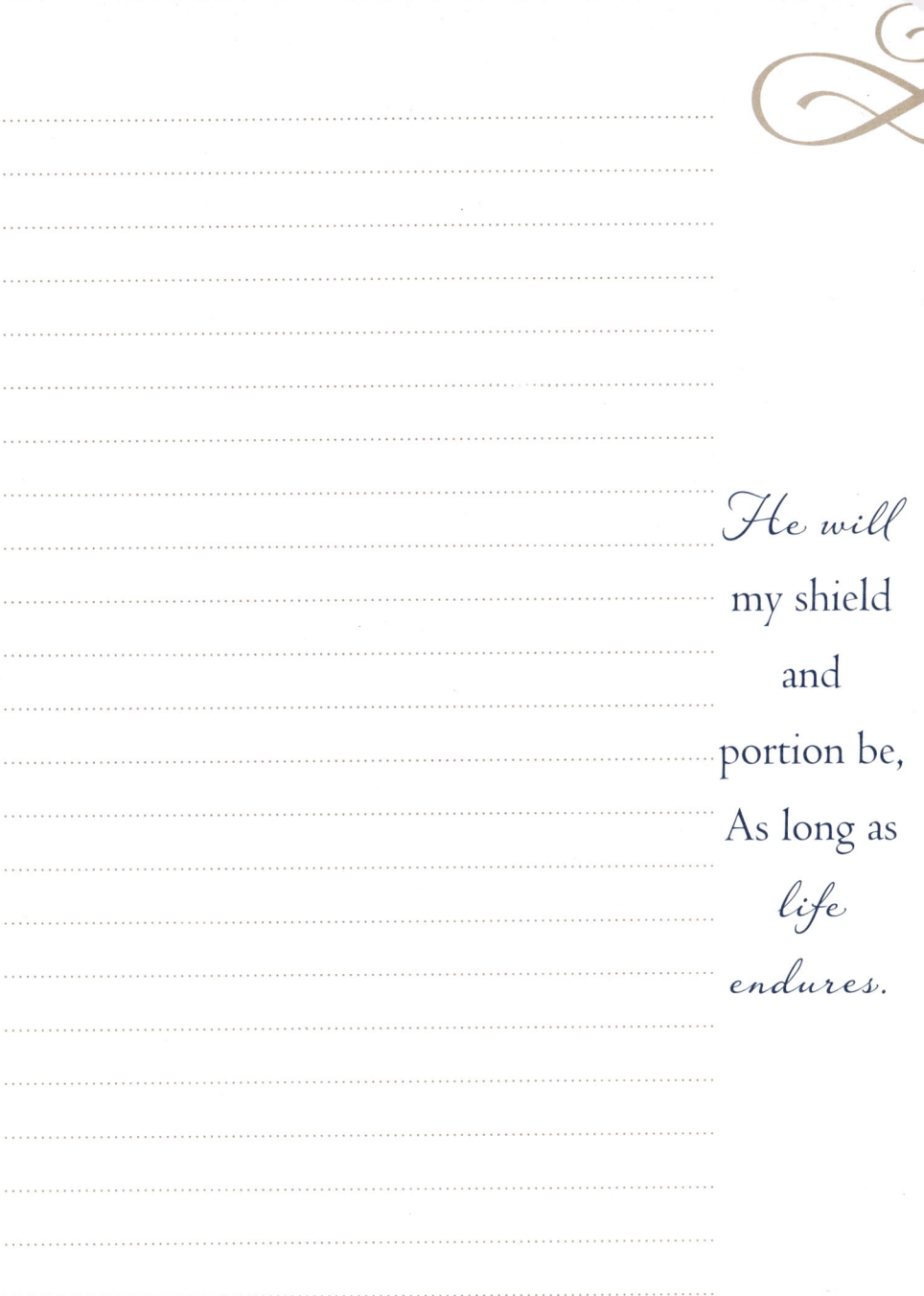

He will my shield and portion be, As long as life endures.

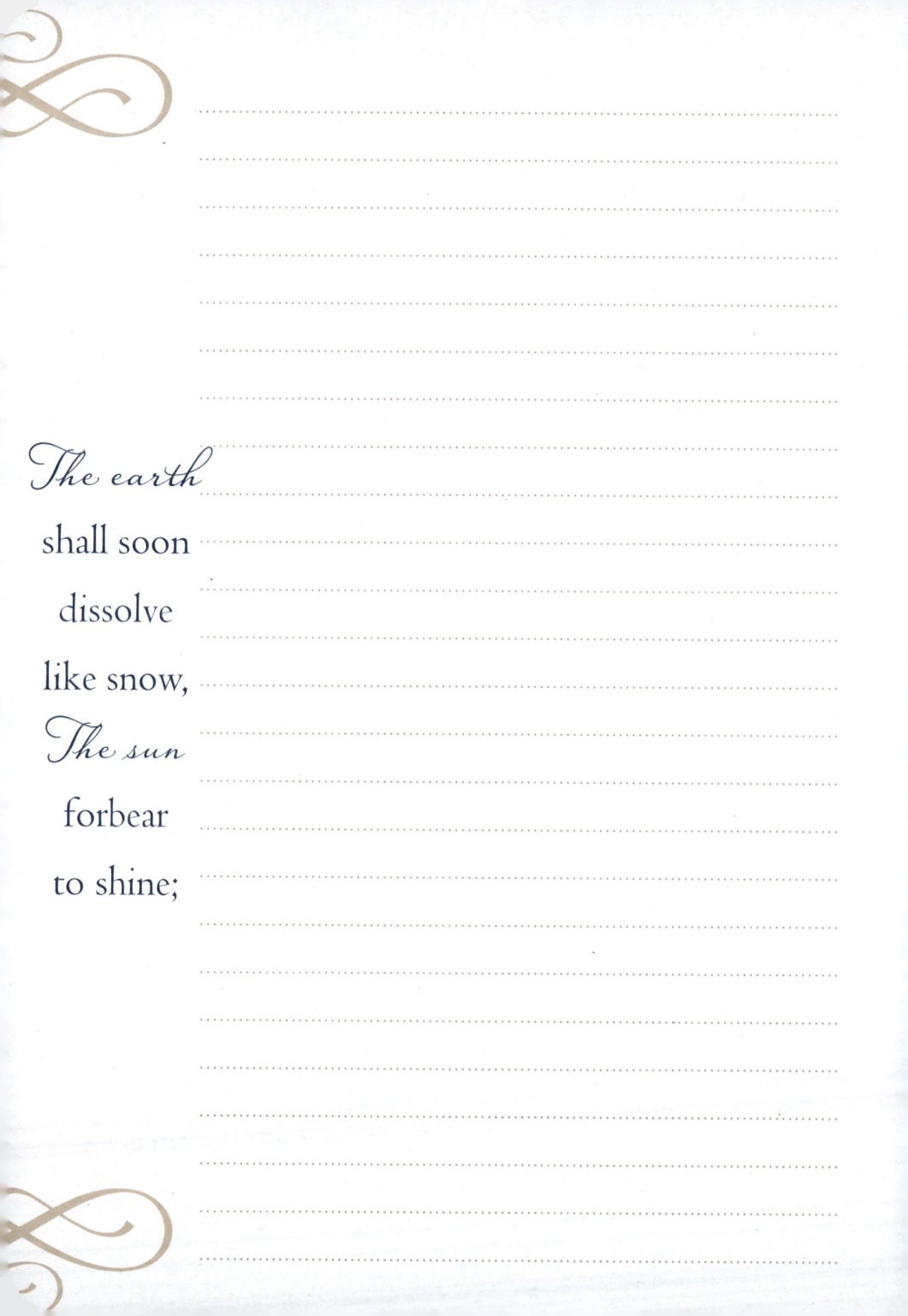

The earth shall soon dissolve like snow,
The sun forbear to shine;

But God, who called me here below, Will be forever mine.

> When we've been there ten thousand years,
> *Bright shining* as the sun;

We've no less days *to sing God's praise* Than when we'd first begun.

Amazing grace, how sweet the sound, That saved a wretch like me!

I once *was lost* but now am found, *Was blind* but now I see.

'Twas grace that taught my heart to fear, And grace my fears relieved;

How *precious* did that *grace* appear The hour *I first believed!*

Through many dangers, toils, and snares, I have already come;

'Twas *grace* that brought me safe thus far, *And grace* will lead me home.

The Lord has promised good to me. His Word my hope secures.

He will my shield and portion be, As long as life endures.

The earth
shall soon
dissolve
like snow,
The sun
forbear
to shine;

*But God,
who called
me here
below,
Will be
forever
mine.*

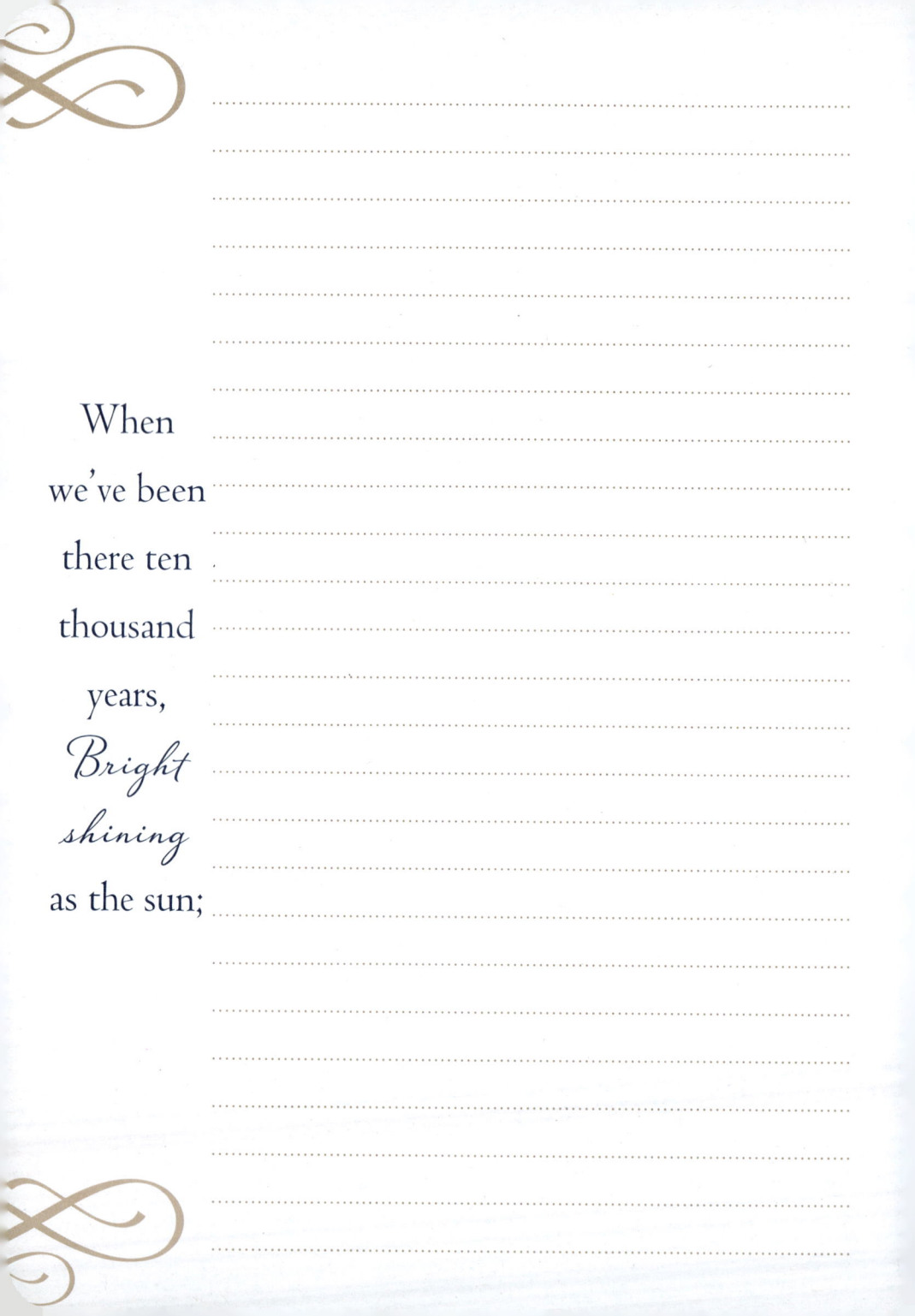

When
we've been
there ten
thousand
years,
Bright
shining
as the sun;

We've no less days *to sing God's praise* Than when we'd first begun.

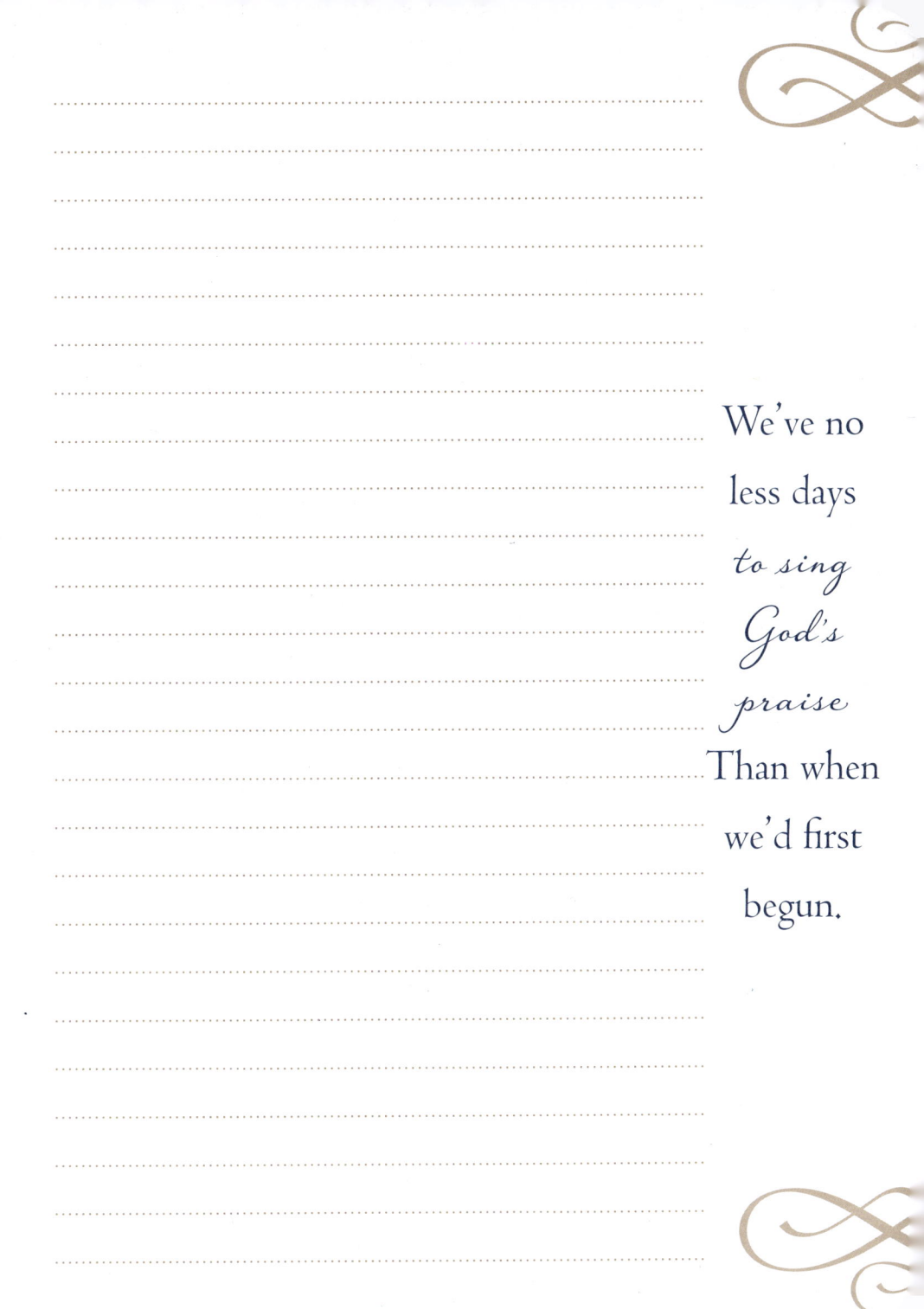

Amazing grace, how sweet the sound, That saved a wretch like me!

I once *was lost* but now am found, *Was blind* but now I see.

'Twas grace that taught my heart to fear, And grace my fears relieved;

How precious did that grace appear The hour I first believed!

Through many dangers, *toils, and snares,* I have already come;

'Twas *grace* that brought me safe thus far, *And* *grace* will lead me home.

The Lord has promised good to me. His Word my hope secures.

He will my shield and portion be, As long as life endures.

The earth shall soon dissolve like snow, The sun forbear to shine;

But God, who called me here below, Will be forever mine.

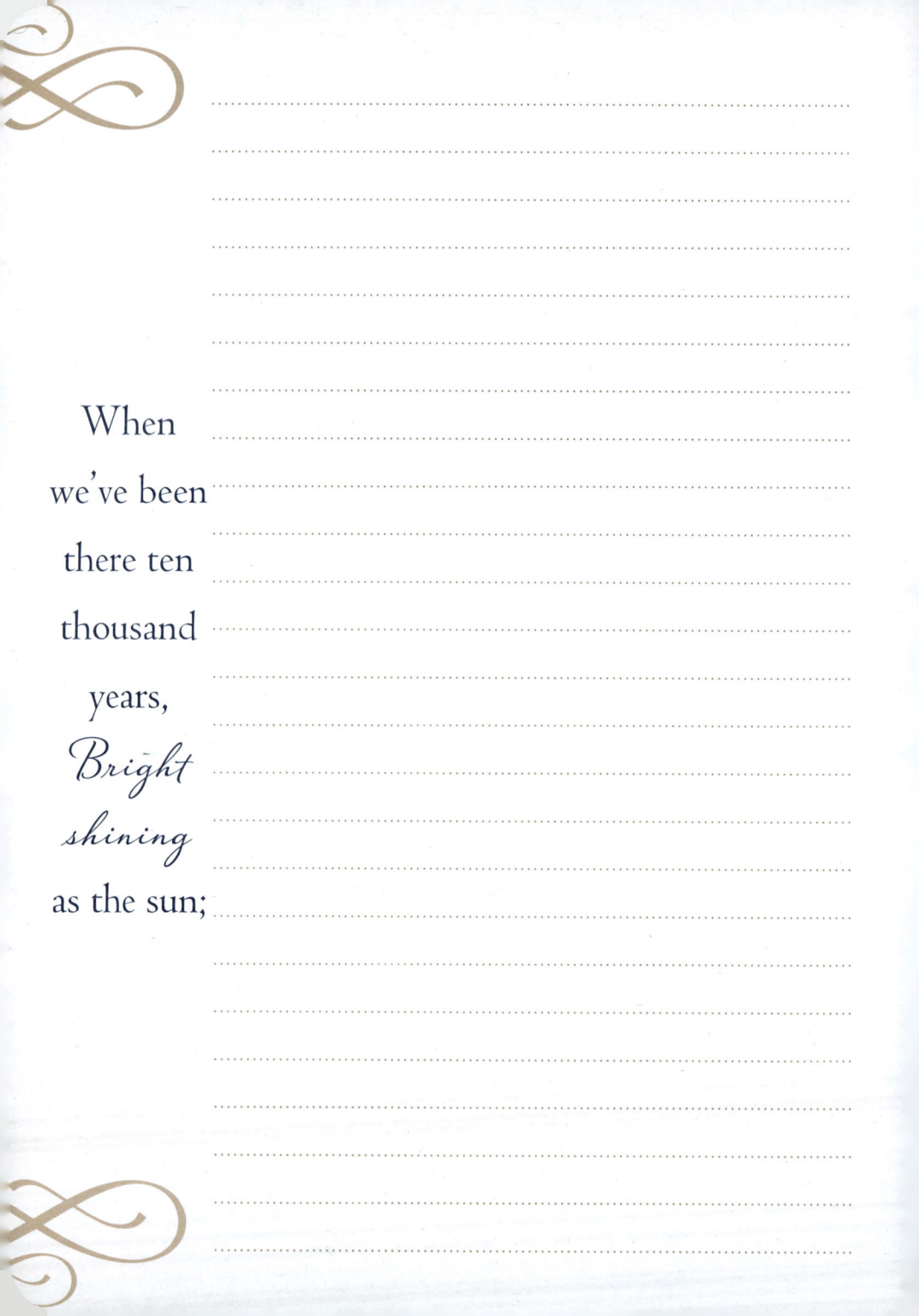

When we've been there ten thousand years,
Bright shining as the sun;

> We've no less days *to sing God's praise* Than when we'd first begun.

Amazing grace, how sweet the sound, That saved a wretch like me!

> I once *was lost* but now am found, *Was blind* but now I see.

'Twas grace that taught my heart to fear, And grace my fears relieved;

How *precious* did that *grace* appear The hour *I first believed!*

Through many dangers, toils, and snares, I have already come;

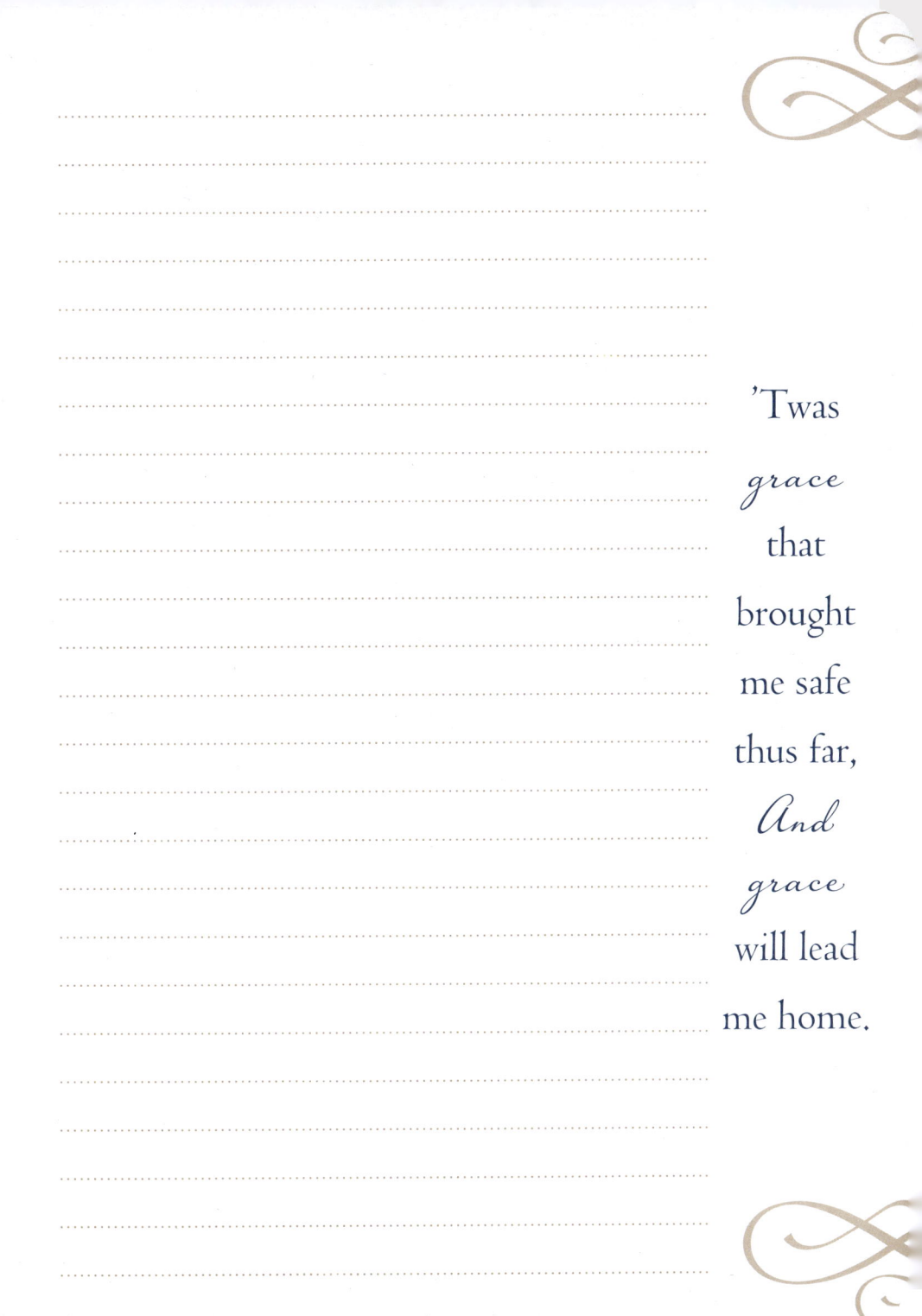

'Twas *grace* that brought me safe thus far, *And* *grace* will lead me home.

The Lord has promised good to me. His Word my hope secures.

He will my shield and portion be, As long as life endures.

The earth shall soon dissolve like snow, The sun forbear to shine;

But God, who called me here below, Will be forever mine.

When we've been there ten thousand years,
Bright shining as the sun;

We've no less days to sing God's praise Than when we'd first begun.

Amazing
grace,
how sweet
the sound,
That
saved
a wretch
like me!

I once was lost but now am found, Was blind but now I see.

> 'Twas grace that taught my heart to fear, And grace my fears relieved;

How *precious* did that *grace* appear
The hour *I first believed!*

Through many dangers, *toils, and snares,* I have already come;

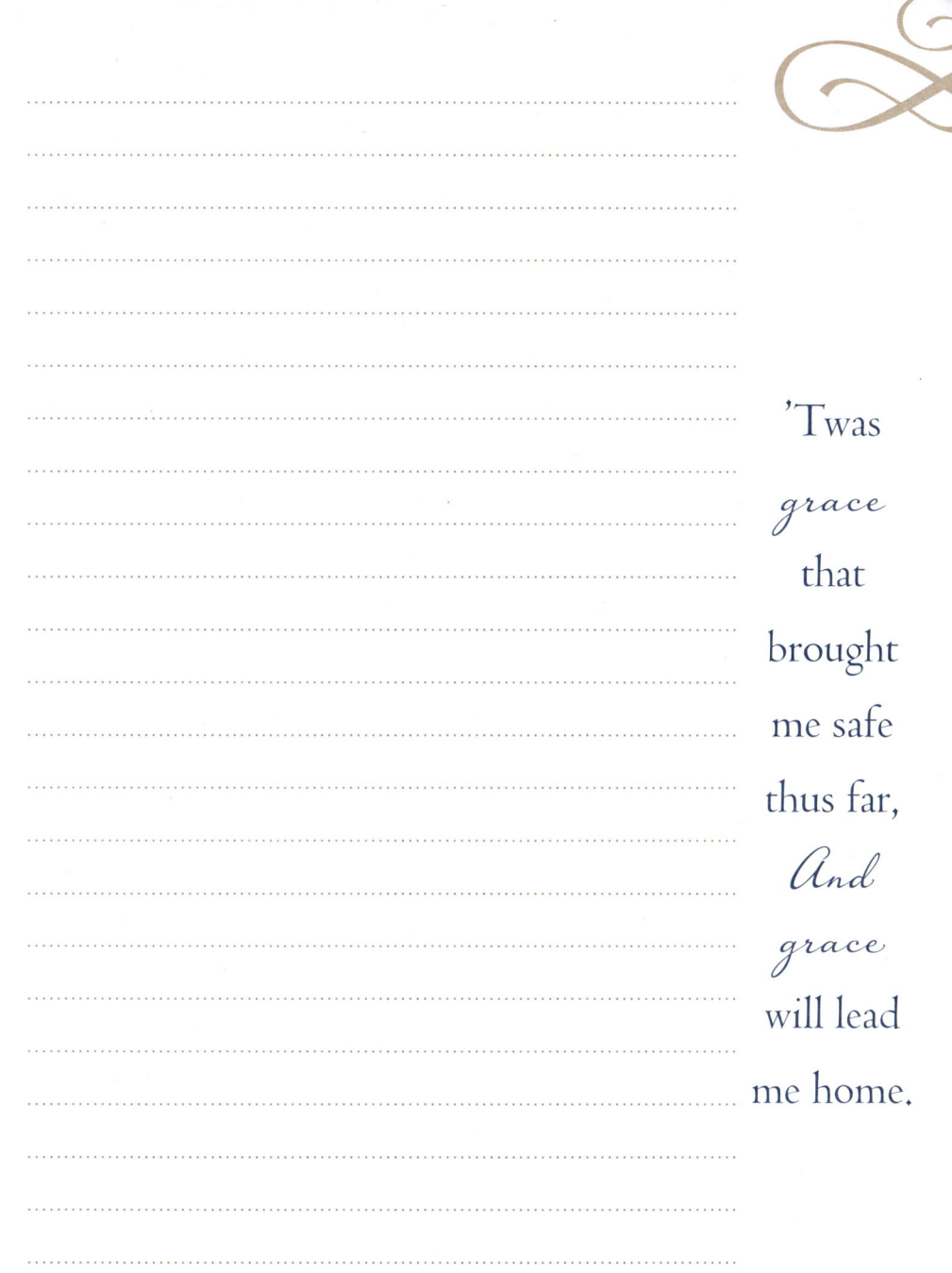

'Twas grace that brought me safe thus far, And grace will lead me home.

The Lord has promised good to me. His Word my hope secures.

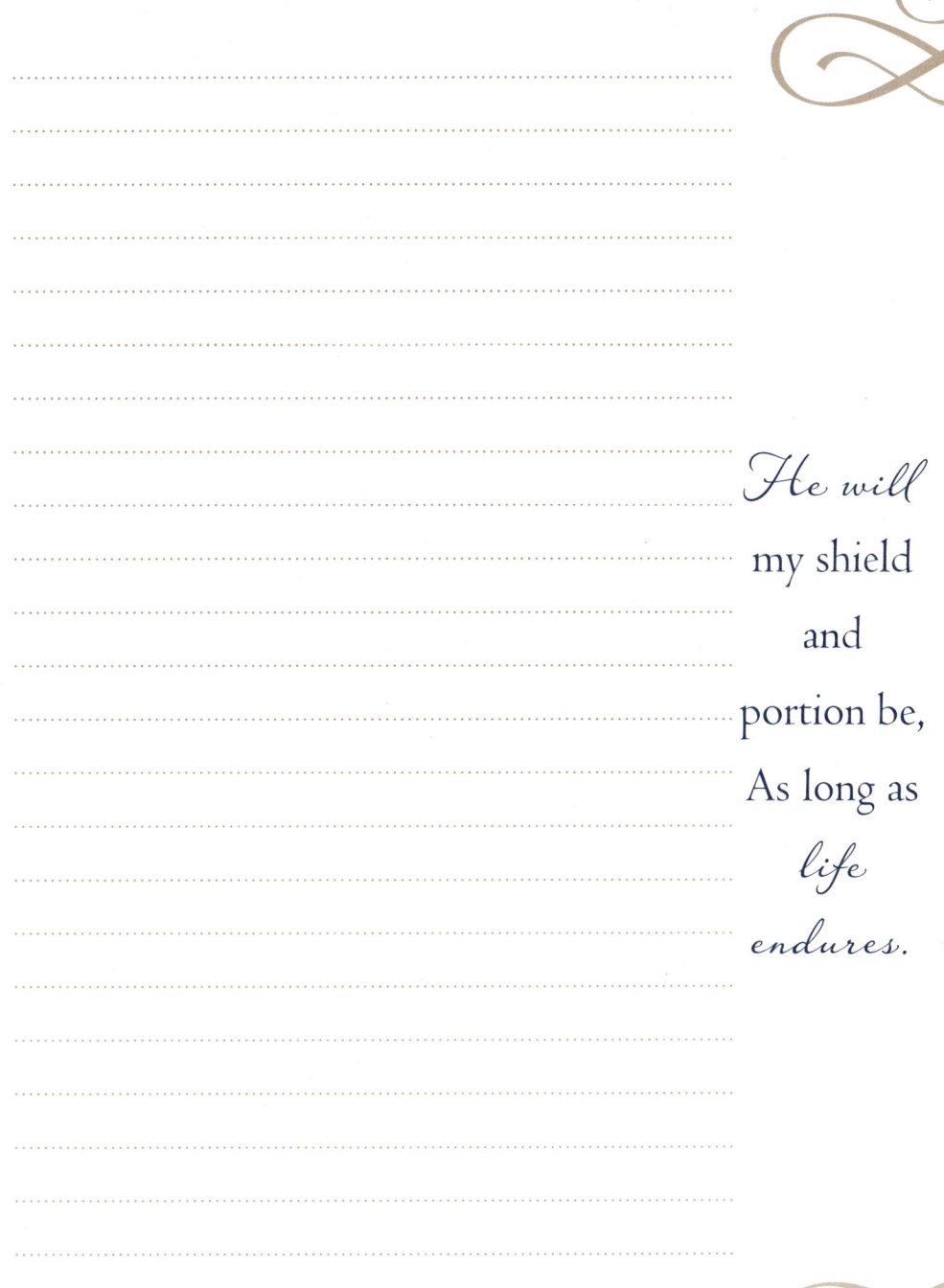

He will my shield and portion be, As long as life endures.

The earth shall soon dissolve like snow, The sun forbear to shine;

But God, who called me here below, Will be forever mine.

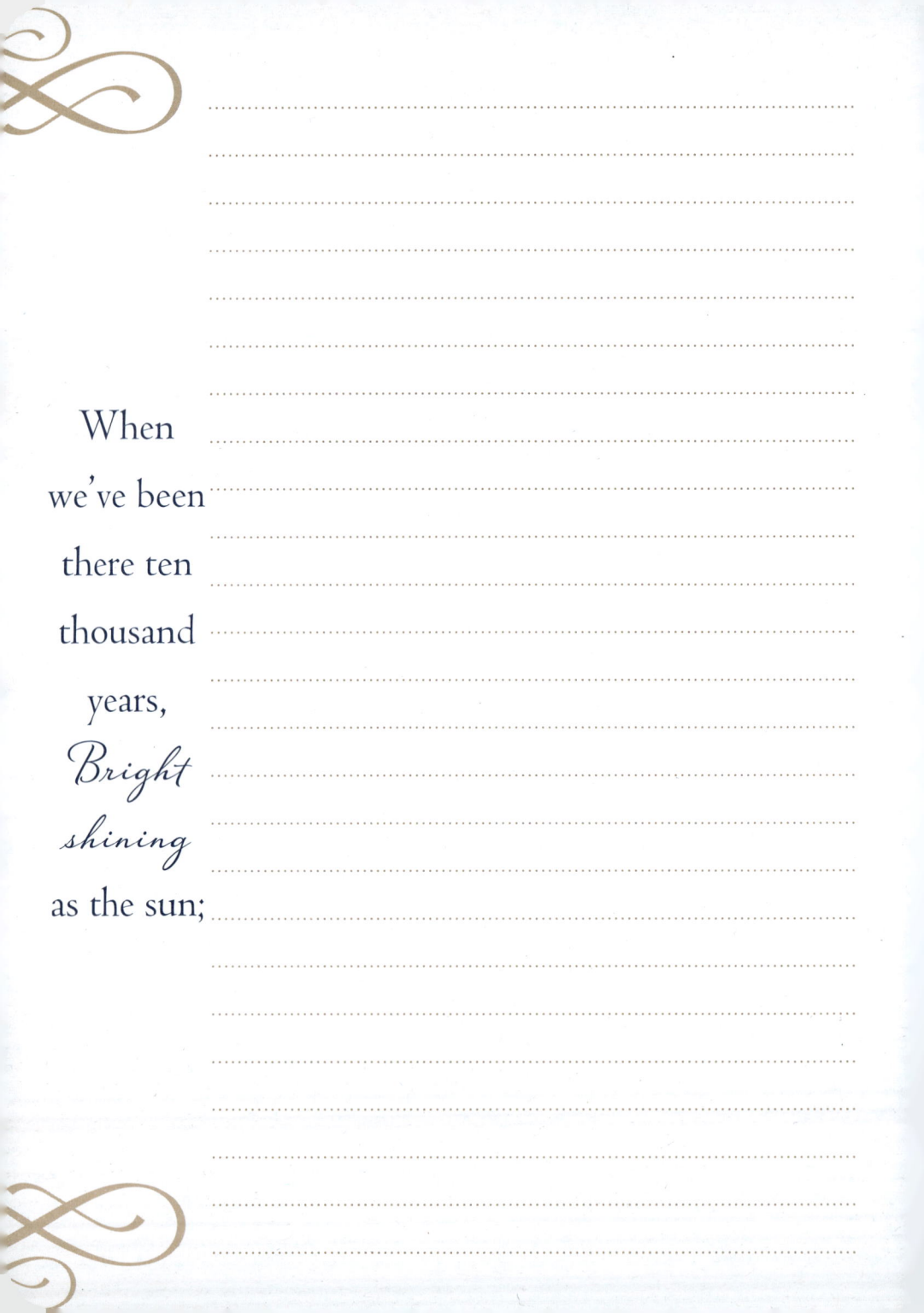

When we've been there ten thousand years, *Bright shining* as the sun;

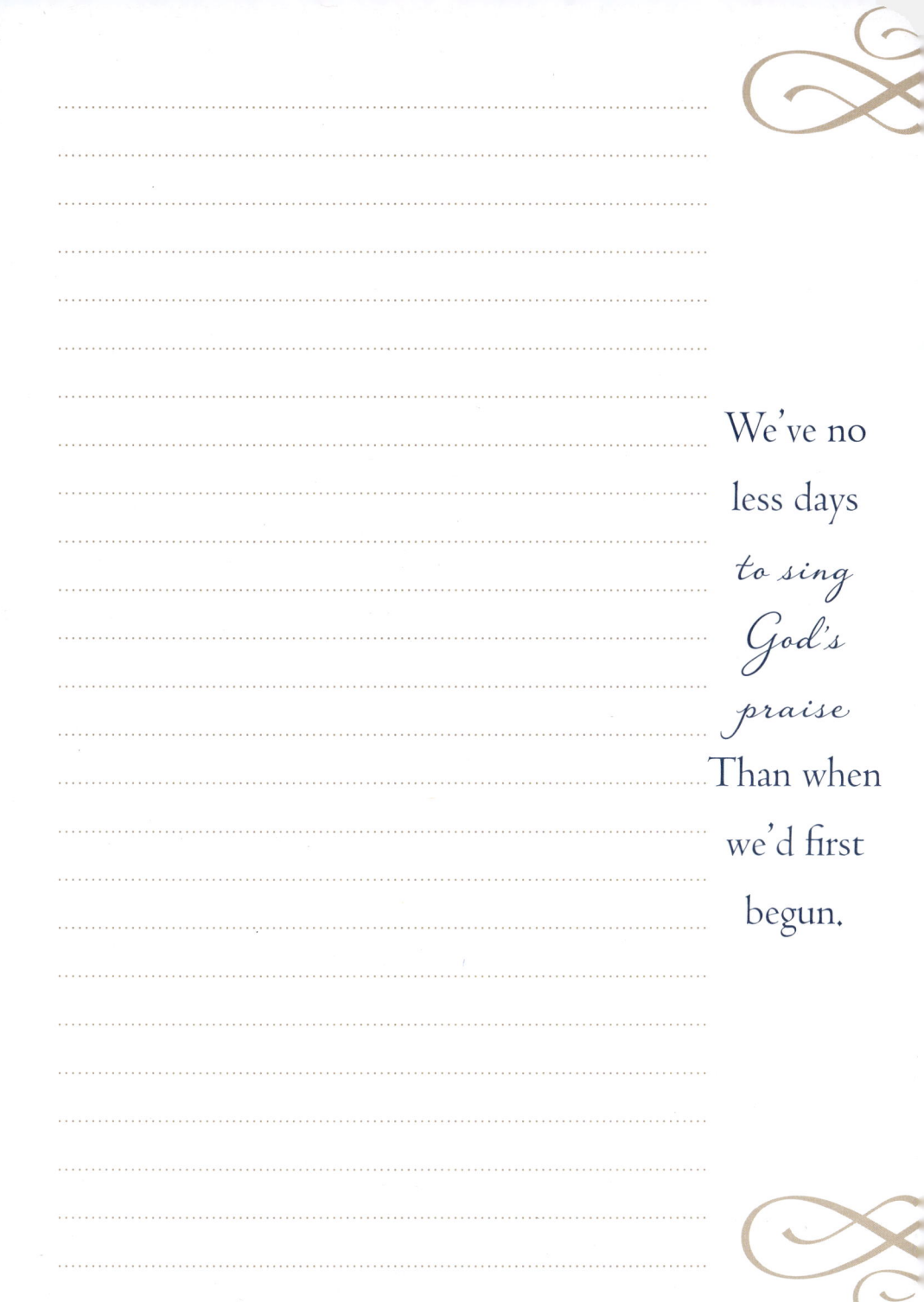

We've no less days to sing God's praise Than when we'd first begun.

Amazing grace, how sweet the sound, That saved a wretch like me!

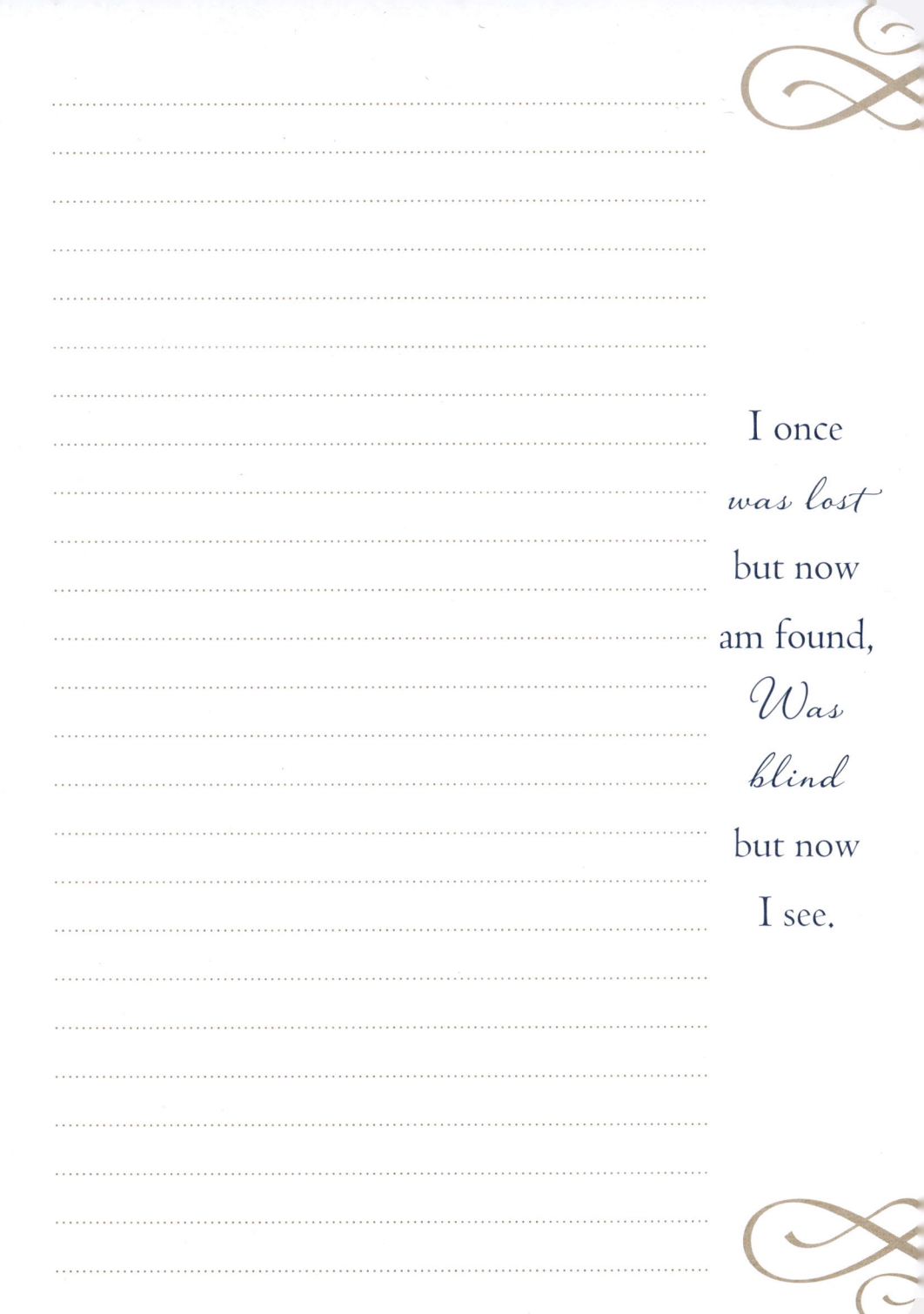

I once was lost but now am found, Was blind but now I see.

'Twas grace that taught my heart to fear, And grace my fears relieved;

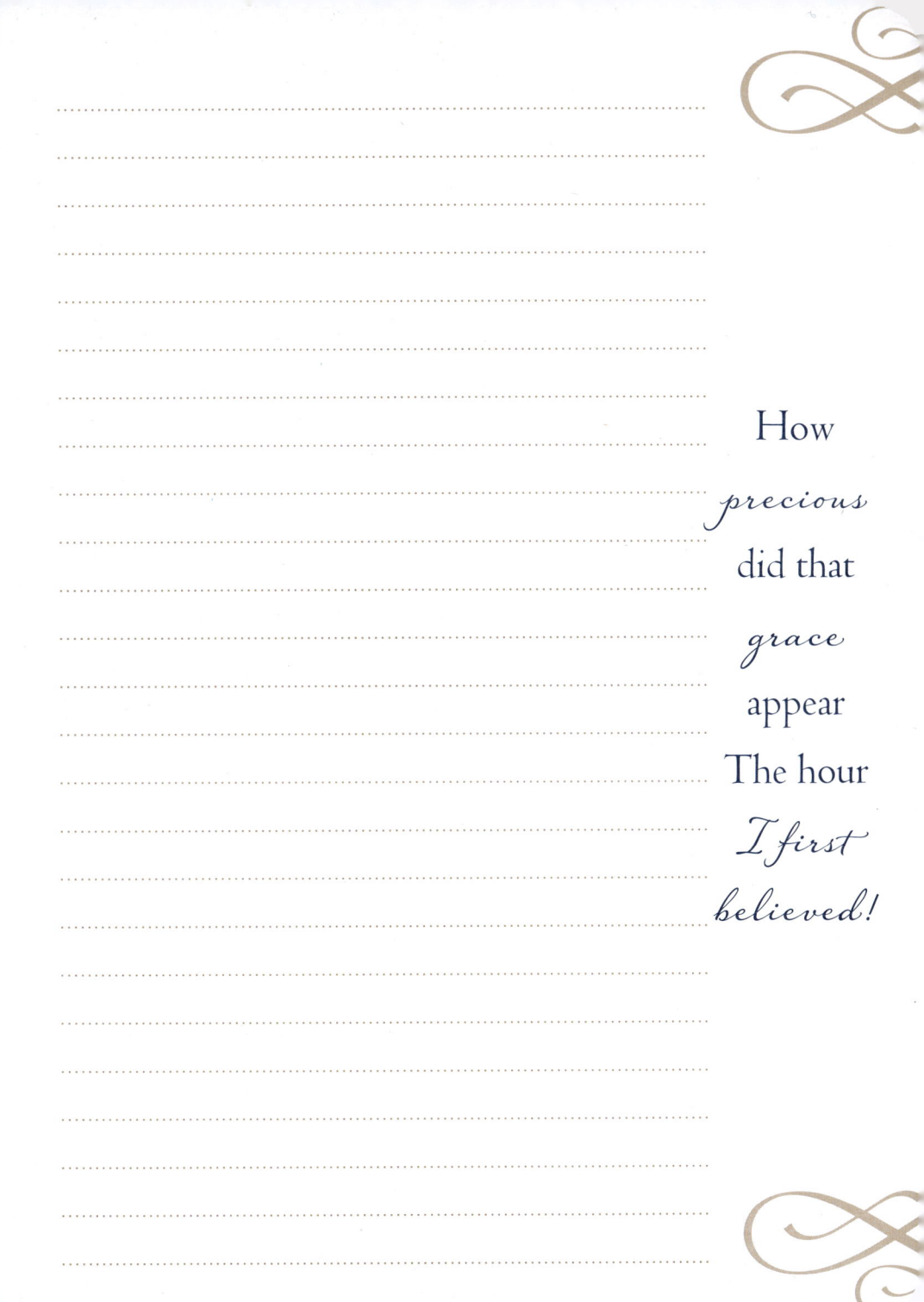

How *precious* did that *grace* appear
The hour *I first believed!*

Through many dangers, *toils, and snares,* I have already come;

'Twas *grace* that brought me safe thus far, *And* *grace* will lead me home.

The Lord has promised good to me. His Word my hope secures.

He will my shield and portion be, As long as life endures.

The earth
shall soon
dissolve
like snow,
The sun
forbear
to shine;

But God, who called me here below, Will be forever mine.

When
we've been
there ten
thousand
years,
*Bright
shining
as the sun;*

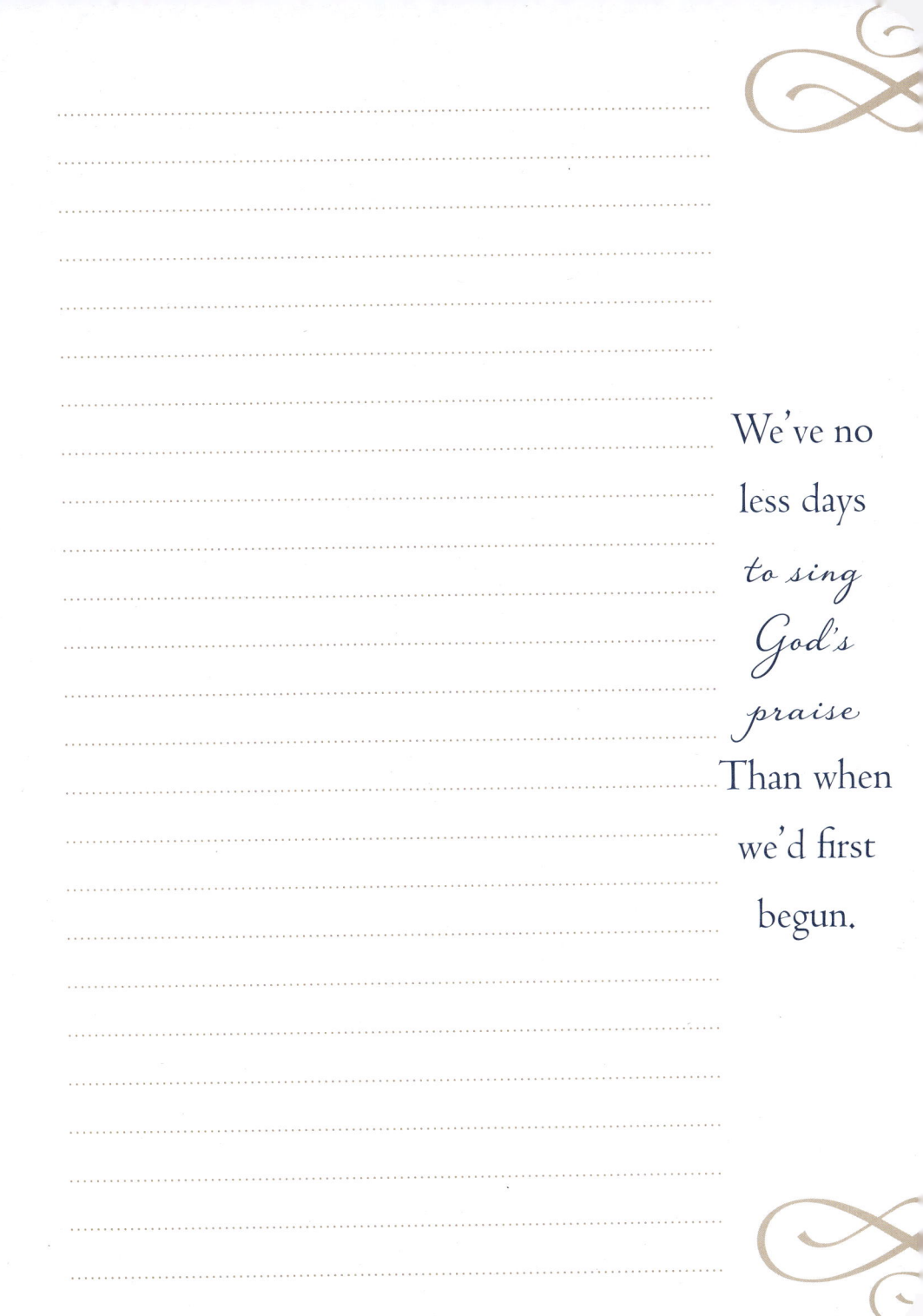

We've no less days *to sing God's praise* Than when we'd first begun.

Amazing grace, how sweet the sound, That saved a wretch like me!

I once was lost but now am found, Was blind but now I see.

'Twas *grace* that taught my heart to fear, *And grace* my fears *relieved;*

How *precious* did that *grace* appear The hour *I first believed!*

Through many dangers, toils, and snares, I have already come;

'Twas *grace* that brought me safe thus far, *And* *grace* will lead me home.

The Lord has promised good to me. His Word my hope secures.

He will my shield and portion be, As long as life endures.

The earth shall soon dissolve like snow, The sun forbear to shine;

*But God,
who called
me here
below,
Will be
forever
mine.*

When we've been there ten thousand years, *Bright shining* as the sun;

We've no less days *to sing God's praise* Than when we'd first begun.

Amazing grace, how sweet the sound, That saved a wretch like me!

I once was lost but now am found, Was blind but now I see.

'Twas *grace* that taught my heart to fear, And *grace* my fears *relieved;*

How *precious* did that *grace* appear
The hour *I first believed!*

Through many dangers, *toils, and snares,* I have already come;

'Twas *grace* that brought me safe thus far, *And* *grace* will lead me home.

The Lord has promised good to me. His Word my hope secures.

He will my shield and portion be, As long as life endures.

The earth shall soon dissolve like snow, The sun forbear to shine;

> *But God,*
> *who called*
> *me here*
> *below,*
> *Will be*
> *forever*
> *mine.*

When
we've been
there ten
thousand
years,
*Bright
shining
as the sun;*

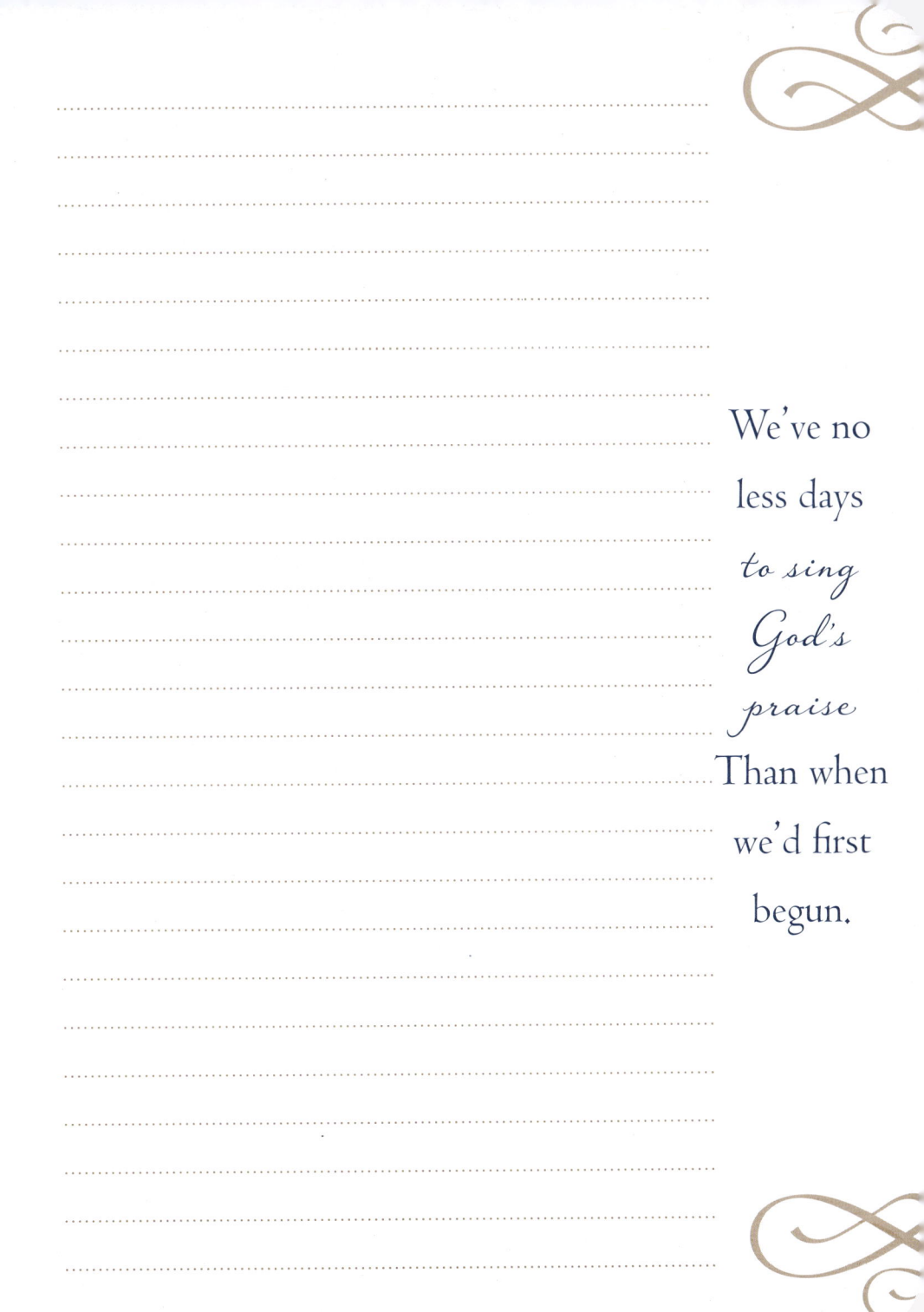

We've no less days to sing God's praise Than when we'd first begun.

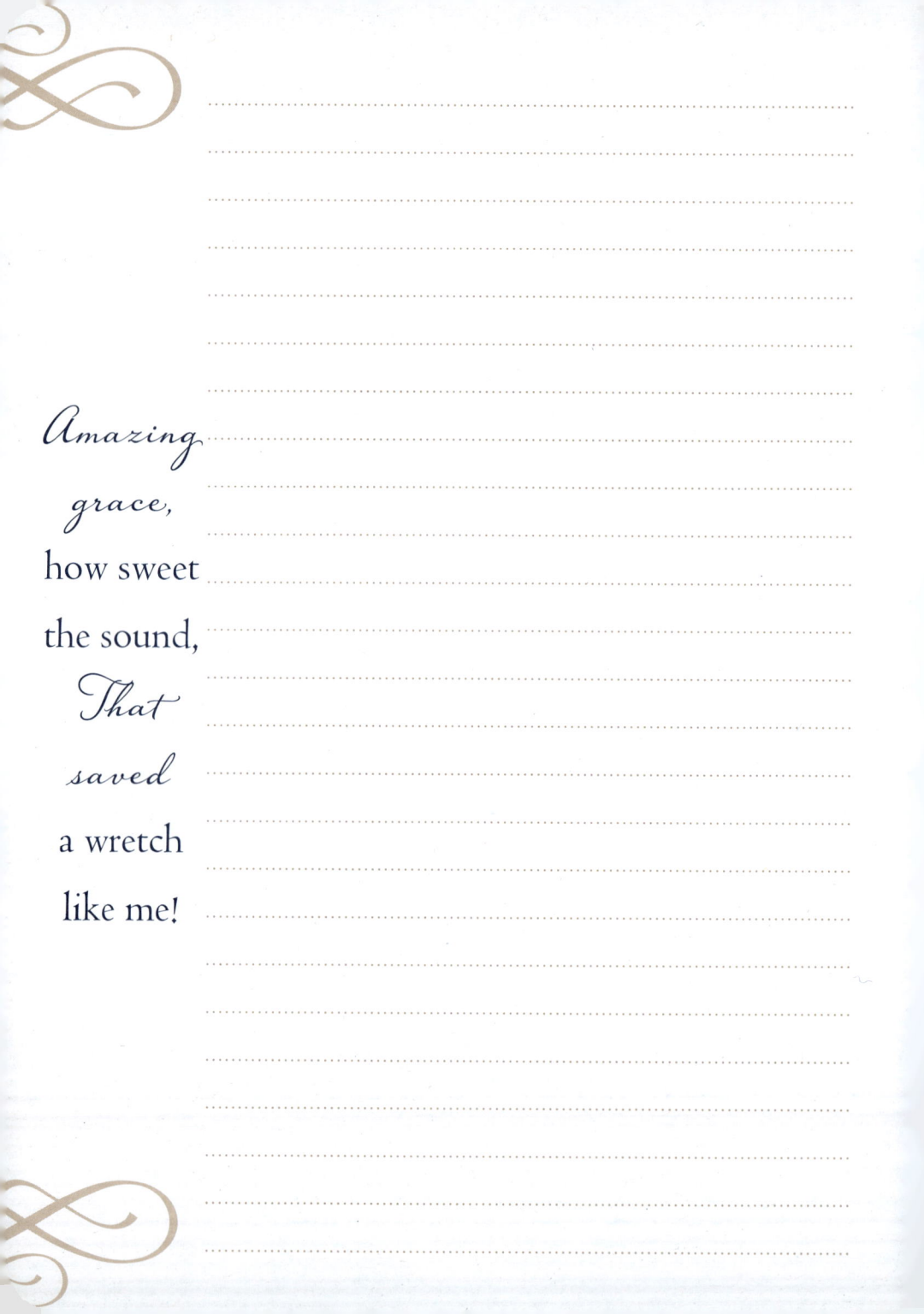

Amazing grace, how sweet the sound, That saved a wretch like me!

I once *was lost* but now am found, *Was blind* but now I see.

'Twas grace that taught my heart to fear, And grace my fears relieved;

How *precious* did that *grace* appear The hour *I first believed!*

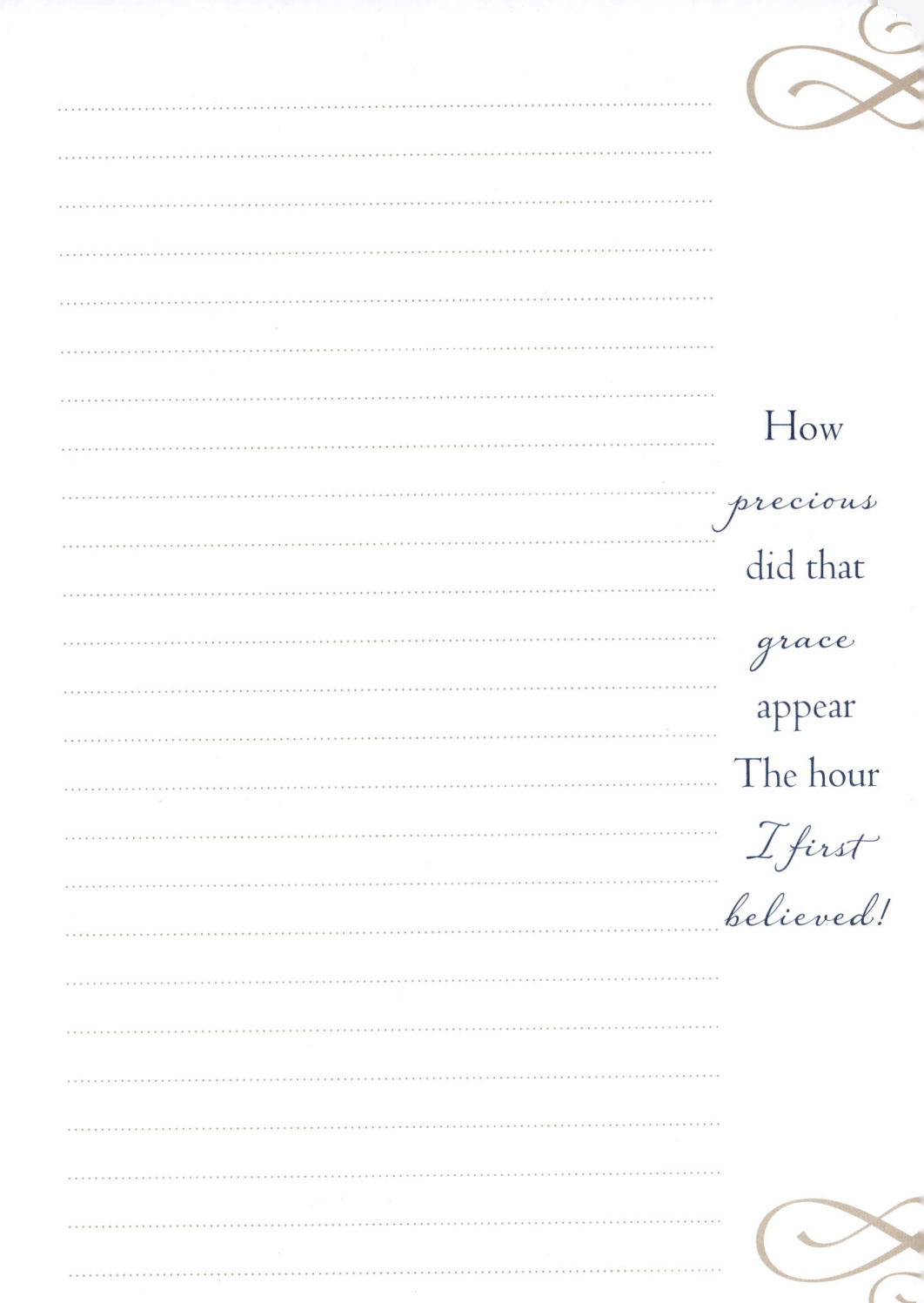

Through many dangers, *toils, and snares,* I have already come;

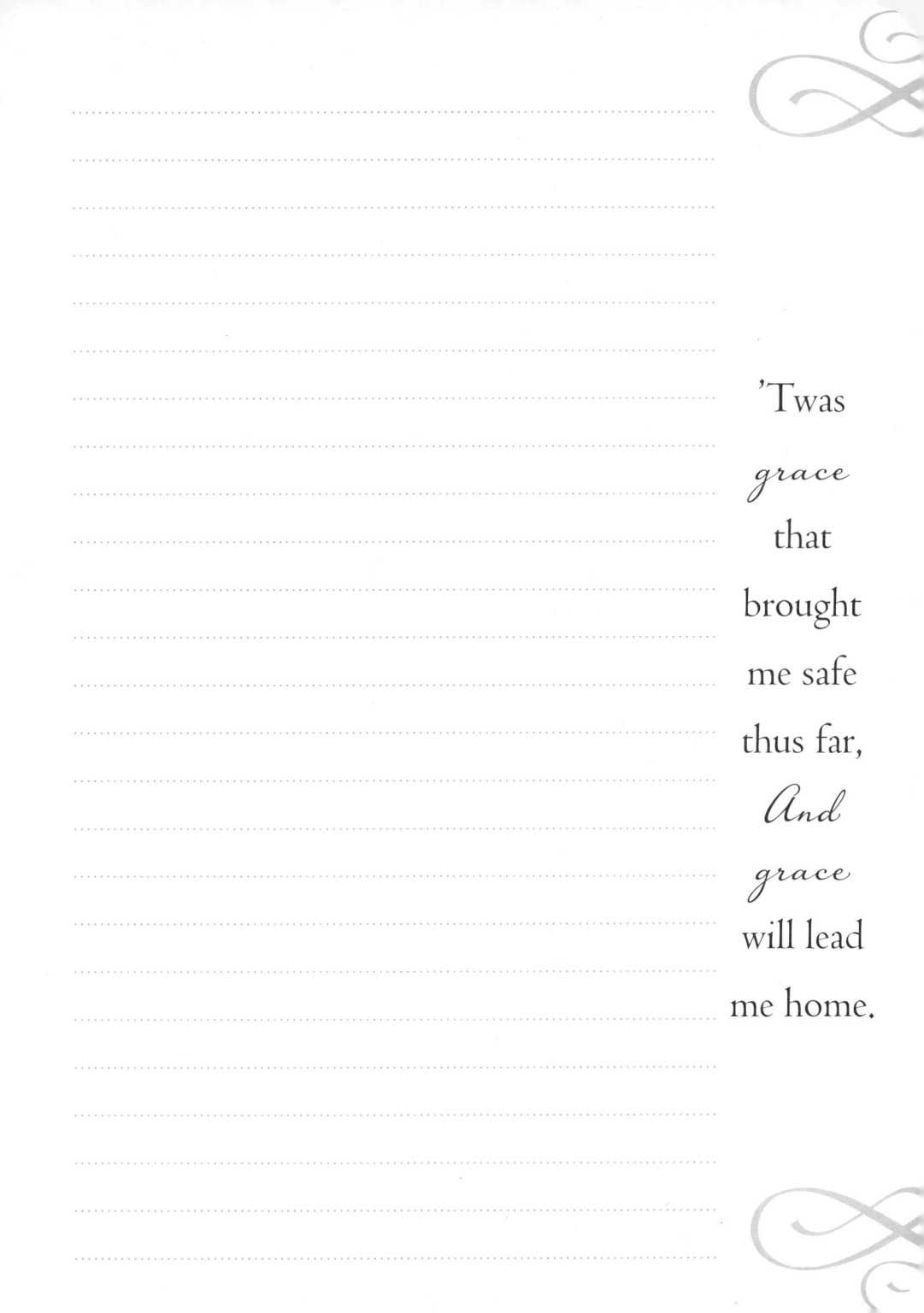

'Twas *grace* that brought me safe thus far, *And grace* will lead me home.

The Lord has promised good to me. His Word my hope secures.

He will my shield and portion be, As long as life endures.

The earth shall soon dissolve like snow, The sun forbear to shine;

> *But God, who called me here below, Will be forever mine.*

When we've been there ten thousand years,
Bright shining as the sun;

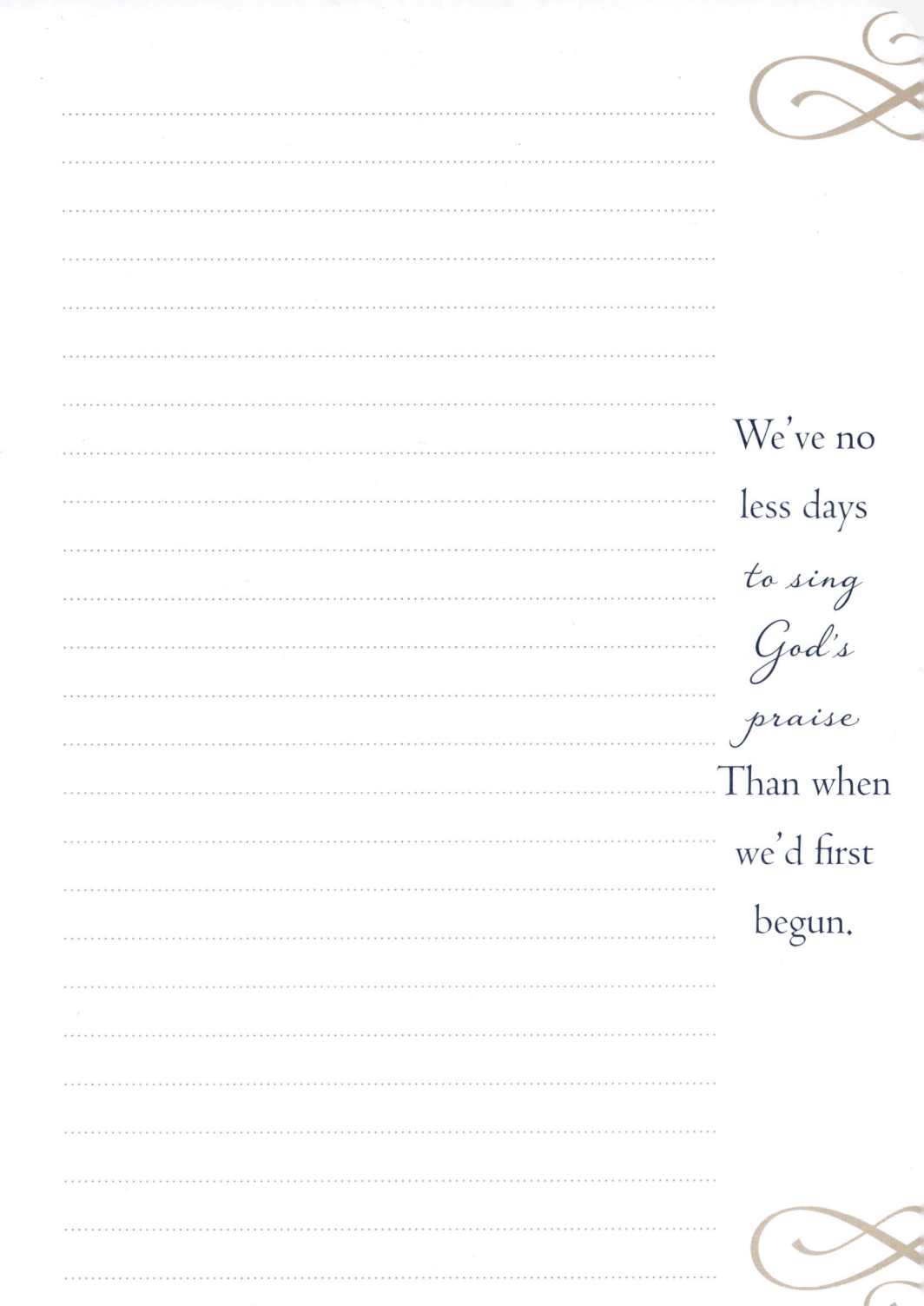

We've no less days *to sing God's praise* Than when we'd first begun.

Amazing grace, how sweet the sound, That saved a wretch like me!

I once was lost but now am found, Was blind but now I see.

'Twas grace that taught my heart to fear, And grace my fears relieved;

How *precious* did that *grace* appear
The hour *I first believed!*

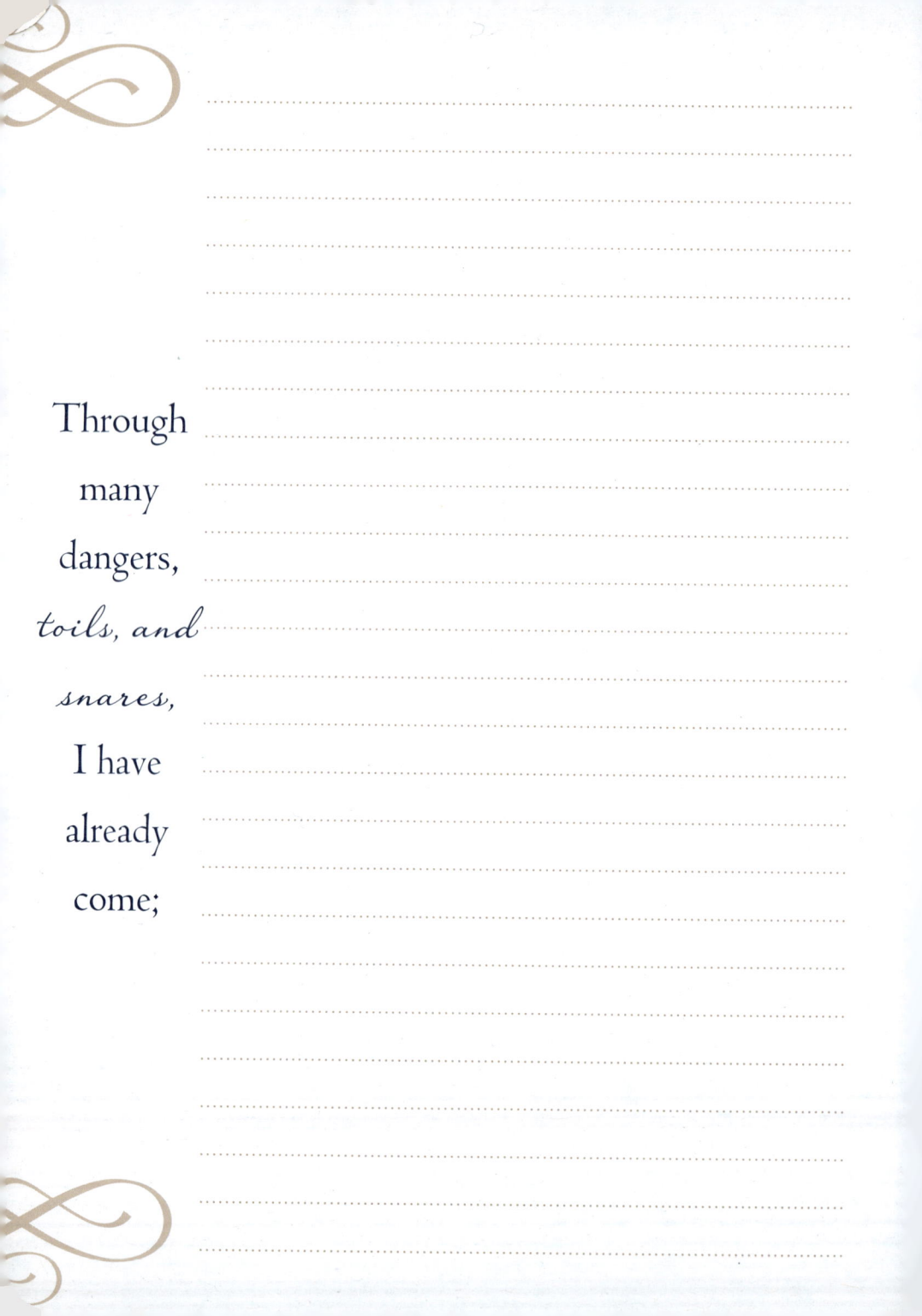

Through many dangers, toils, and snares, I have already come;

'Twas grace that brought me safe thus far, And grace will lead me home.

The Lord has promised good to me. His Word my hope secures.

He will my shield and portion be, As long as life endures.

The earth
shall soon
dissolve
like snow,
The sun
forbear
to shine;

But God, who called me here below, Will be forever mine.

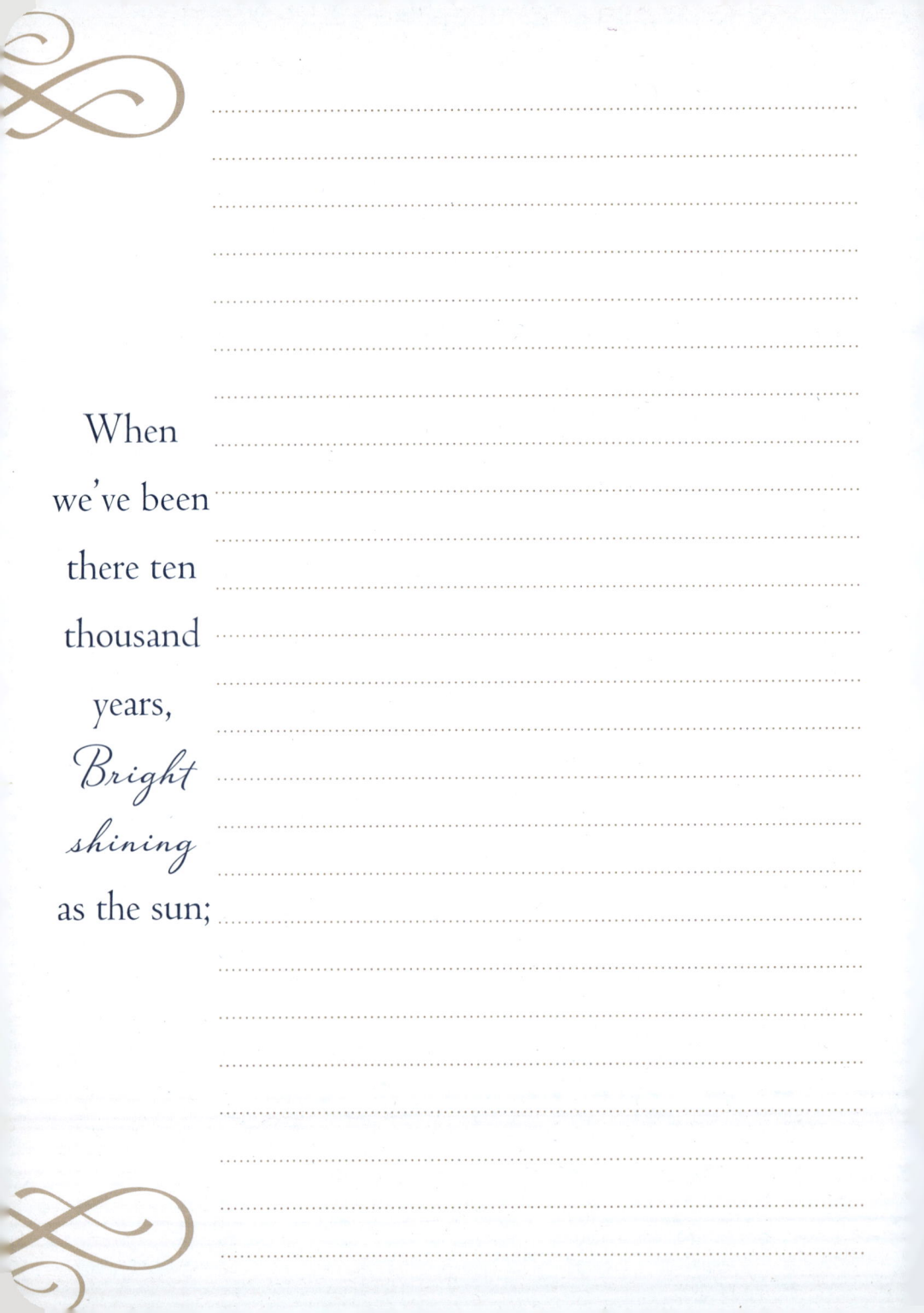

When
we've been
there ten
thousand
years,
Bright
shining
as the sun;

> We've no less days *to sing God's praise* Than when we'd first begun.

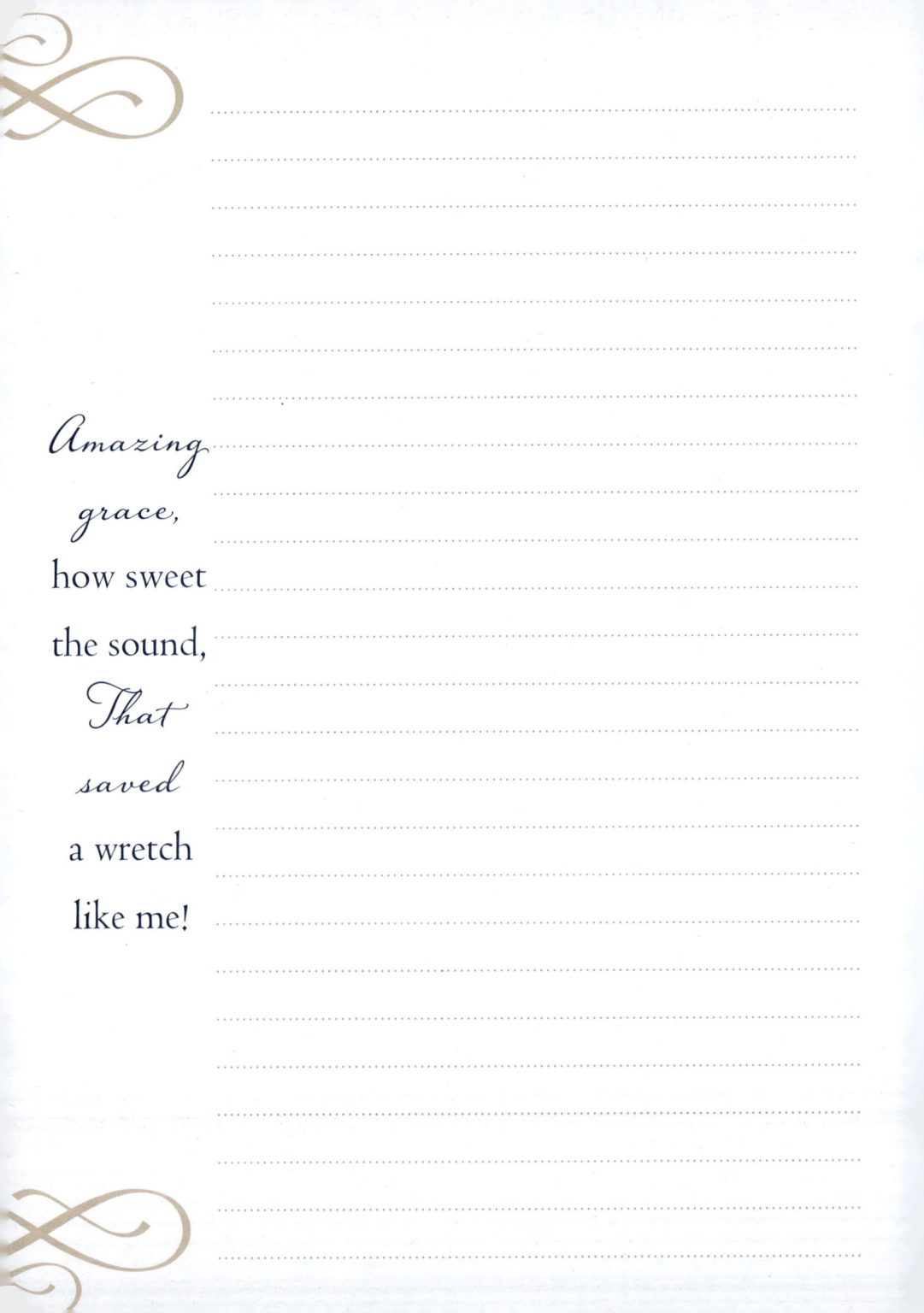

Amazing grace, how sweet the sound, That saved a wretch like me!

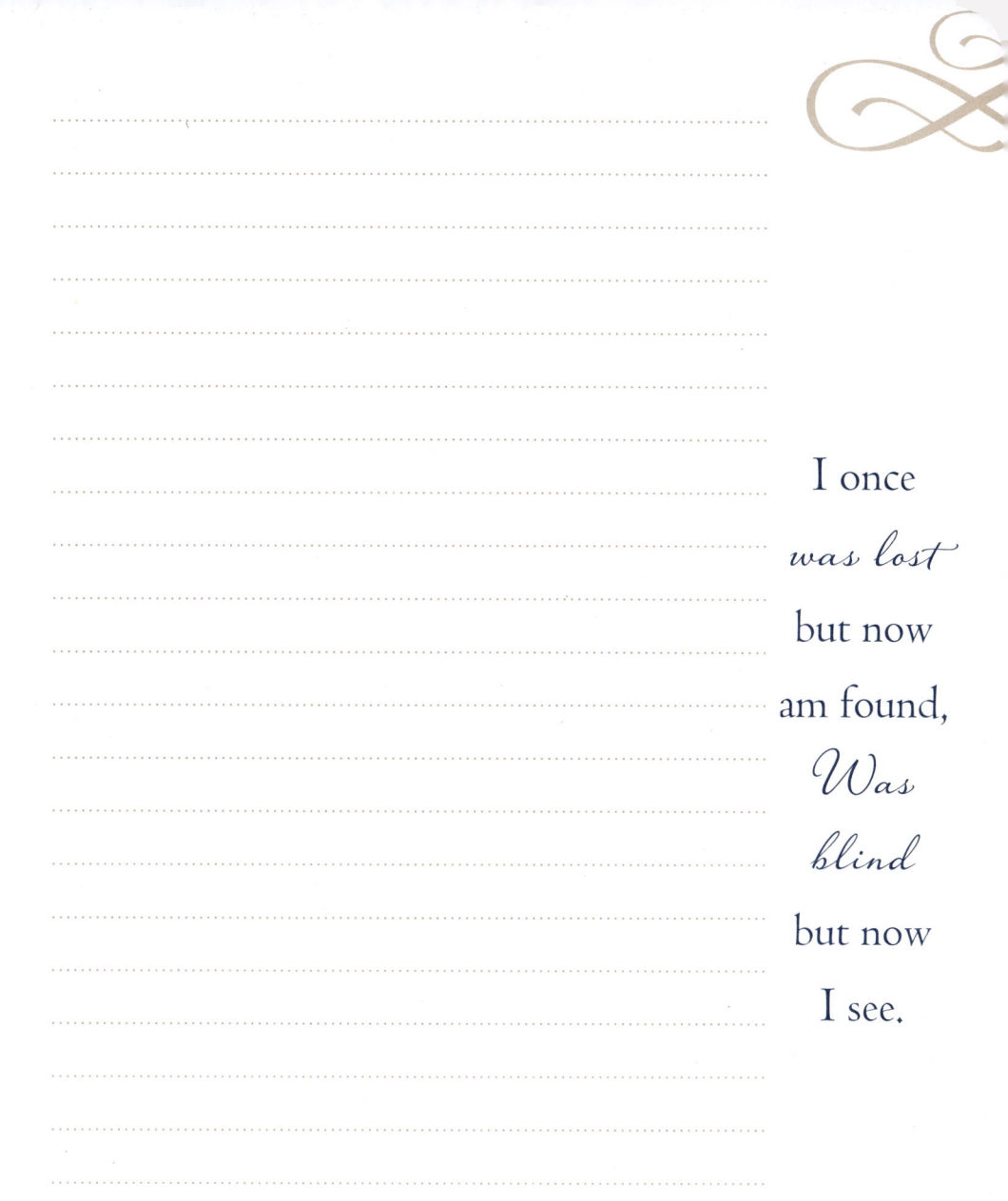

I once was lost but now am found, Was blind but now I see.

'Twas grace that taught my heart to fear, And grace my fears relieved;

How *precious* did that *grace* appear
The hour *I first believed!*

Through many dangers, *toils, and snares,* I have already come;

'Twas *grace* that brought me safe thus far, *And grace* will lead me home.

The Lord has promised good to me. His Word my hope secures.

He will my shield and portion be, As long as life endures.

The earth shall soon dissolve like snow,
The sun forbear to shine;

But God, who called me here below, Will be forever mine.

When
we've been
there ten
thousand
years,
Bright
shining
as the sun;

We've no less days *to sing God's praise* Than when we'd first begun.

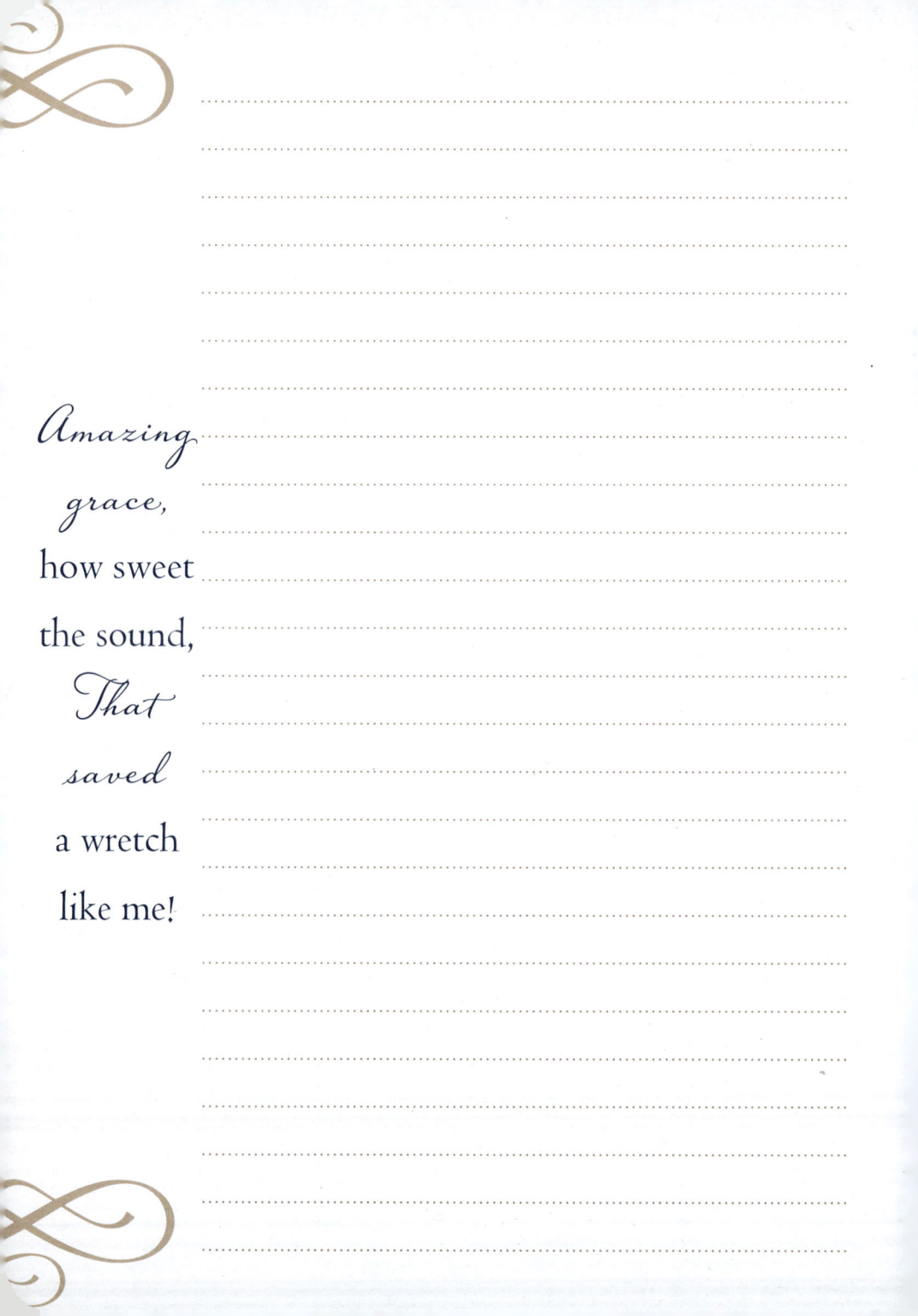

Amazing grace, how sweet the sound, That saved a wretch like me!

I once was lost but now am found, *Was blind* but now I see.

'Twas grace that taught my heart to fear, And grace my fears relieved;

How *precious* did that *grace* appear
The hour *I first believed!*

Through many dangers, toils, and snares, I have already come;

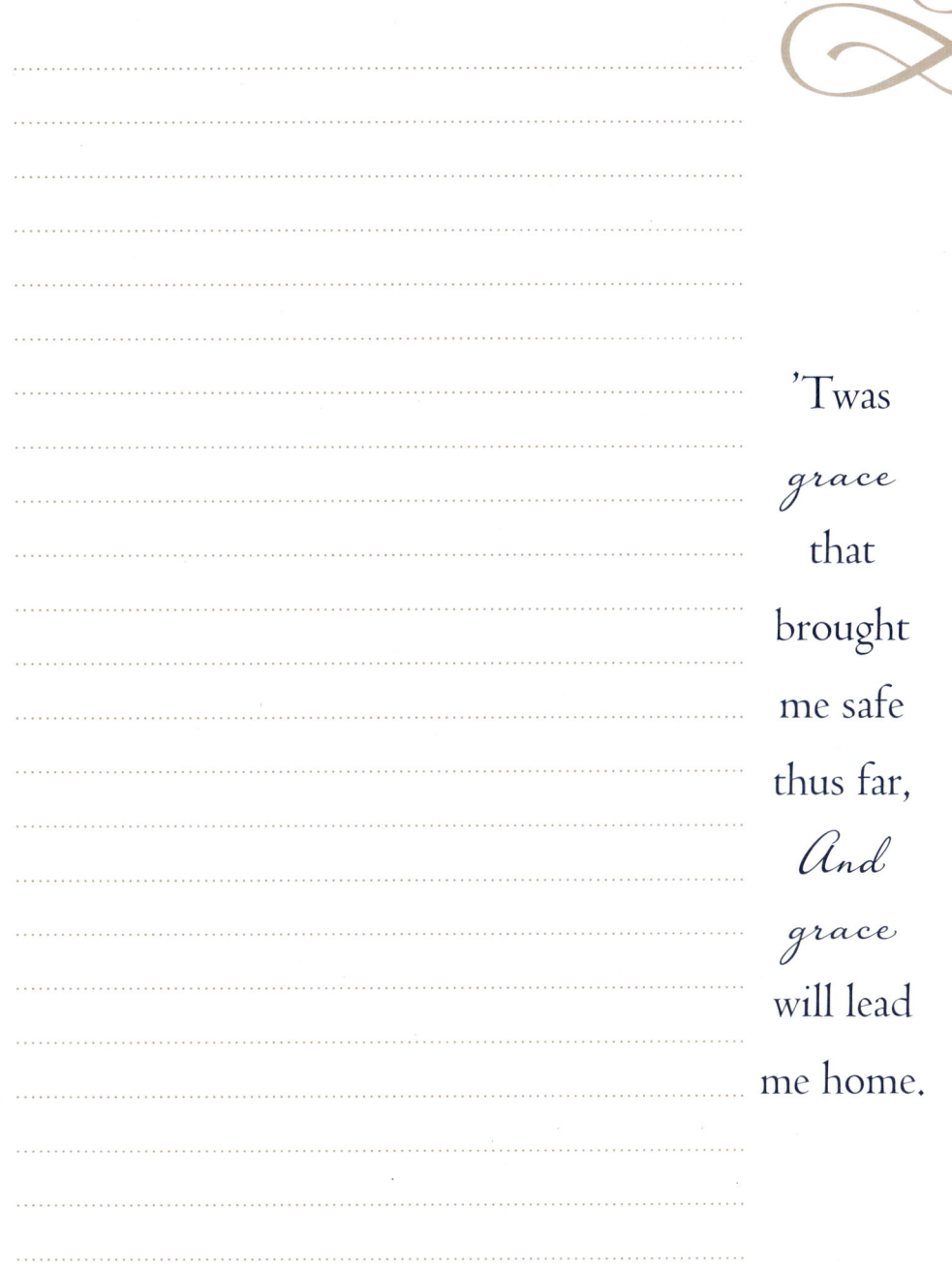

'Twas *grace* that brought me safe thus far, *And grace* will lead me home.

The Lord has promised good to me. His Word my hope secures.

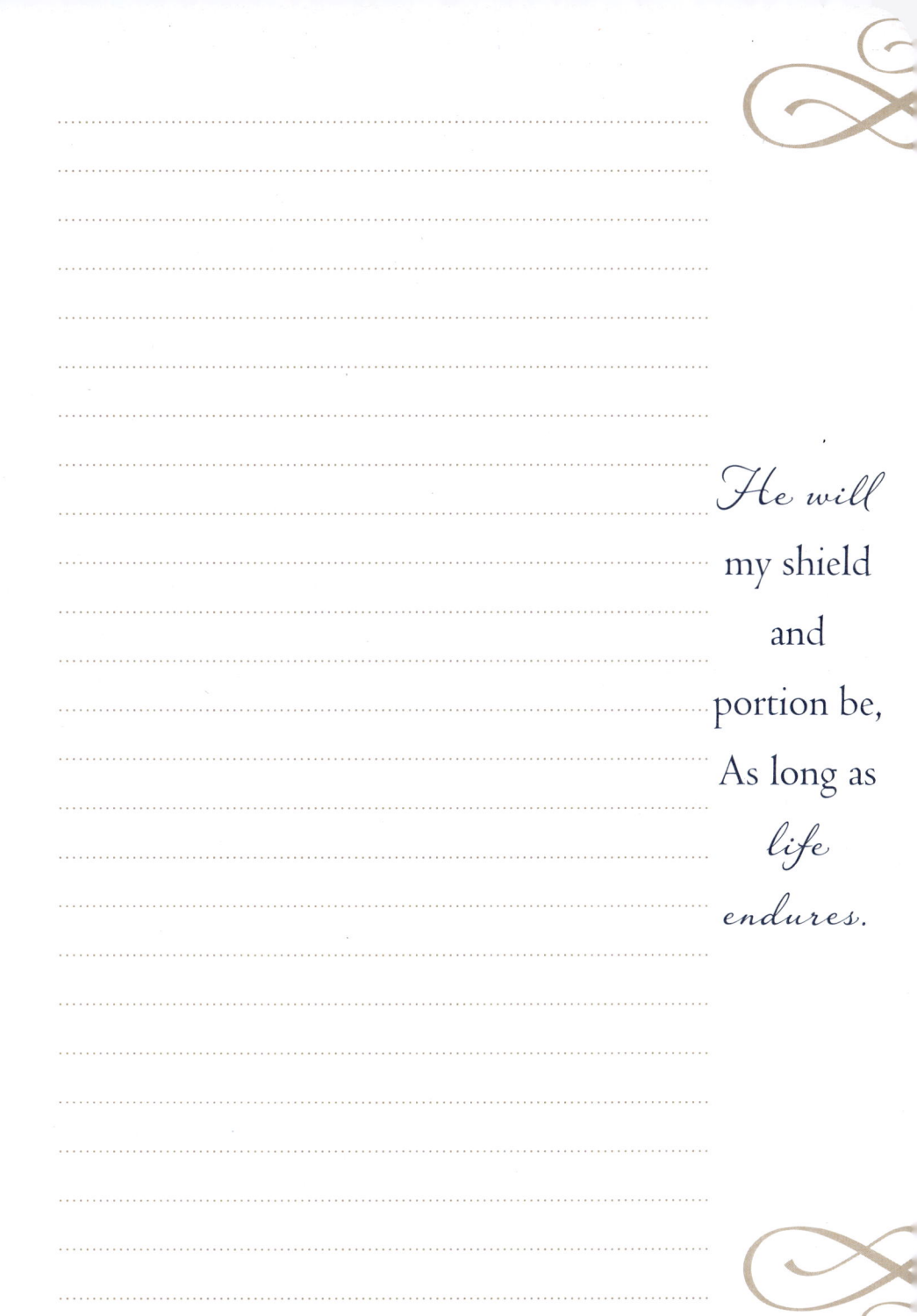

He will my shield and portion be, As long as life endures.

The earth
shall soon
dissolve
like snow,
The sun
forbear
to shine;

> But God,
> who called
> me here
> below,
> Will be
> forever
> mine.

When
we've been
there ten
thousand
years,
Bright
shining
as the sun;

We've no less days *to sing God's praise* Than when we'd first begun.

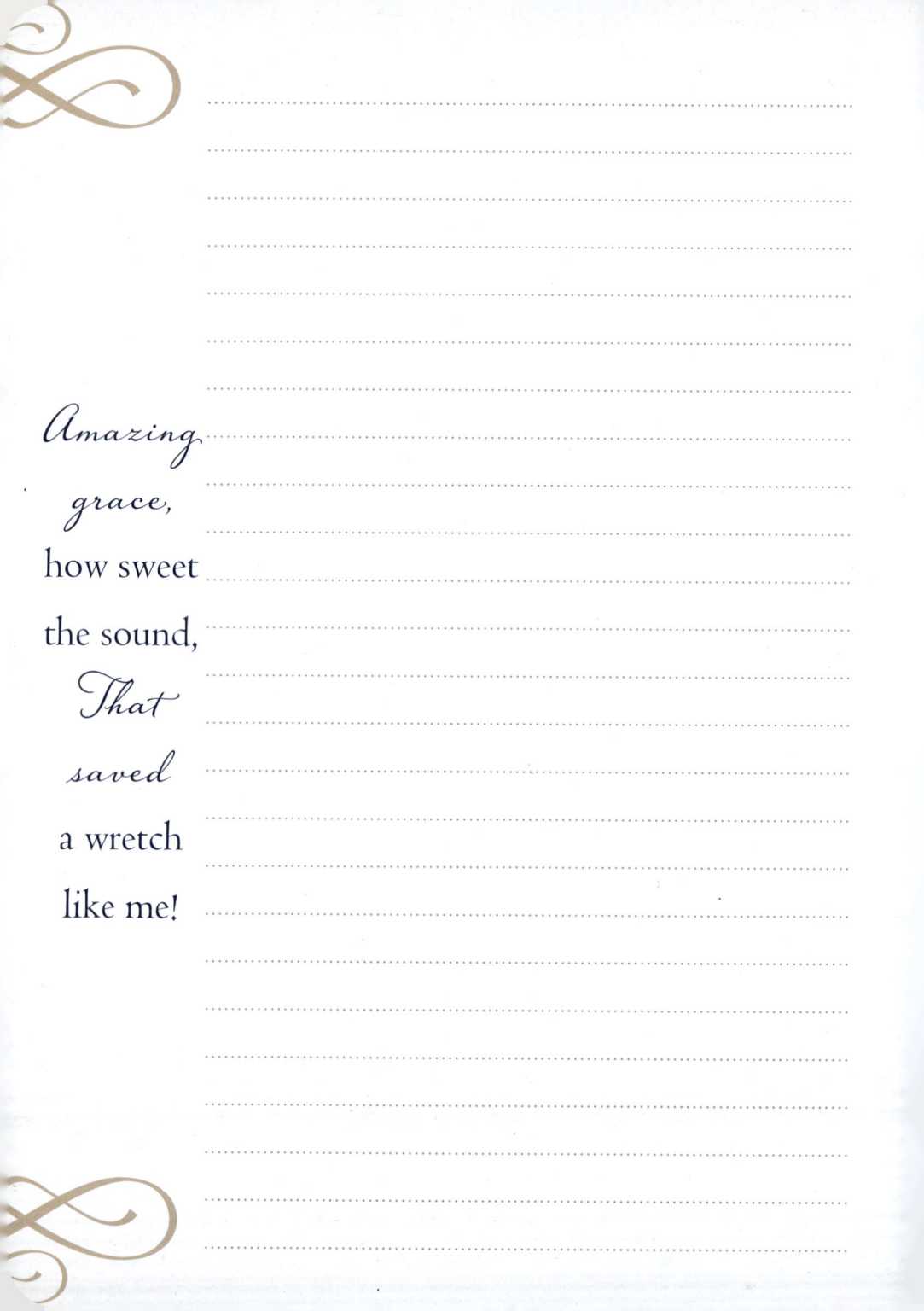

Amazing grace, how sweet the sound, That saved a wretch like me!

I once *was lost* but now am found, *Was blind* but now I see.

'Twas grace that taught my heart to fear, And grace my fears relieved;

> How *precious* did that *grace* appear
> The hour *I first believed!*

Through many dangers, toils, and snares, I have already come;

'Twas *grace* that brought me safe thus far, *And grace* will lead me home.

> The Lord has promised good to me. His Word my hope secures.

He will my shield and portion be, As long as life endures.

The earth shall soon dissolve like snow, The sun forbear to shine;

But God, who called me here below, Will be forever mine.

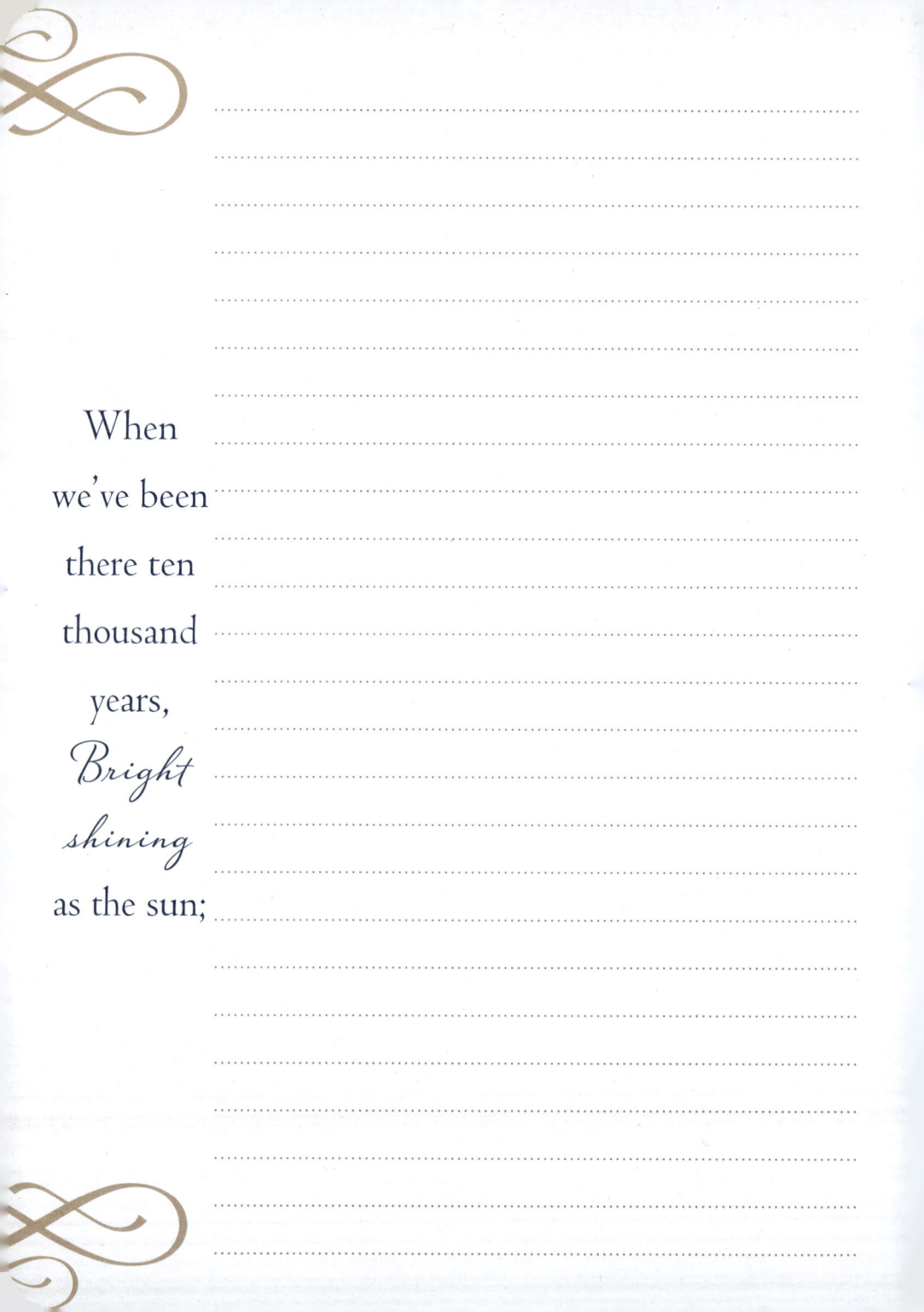

When
we've been
there ten
thousand
years,
*Bright
shining
as the sun;*

We've no less days *to sing God's praise* Than when we'd first begun.

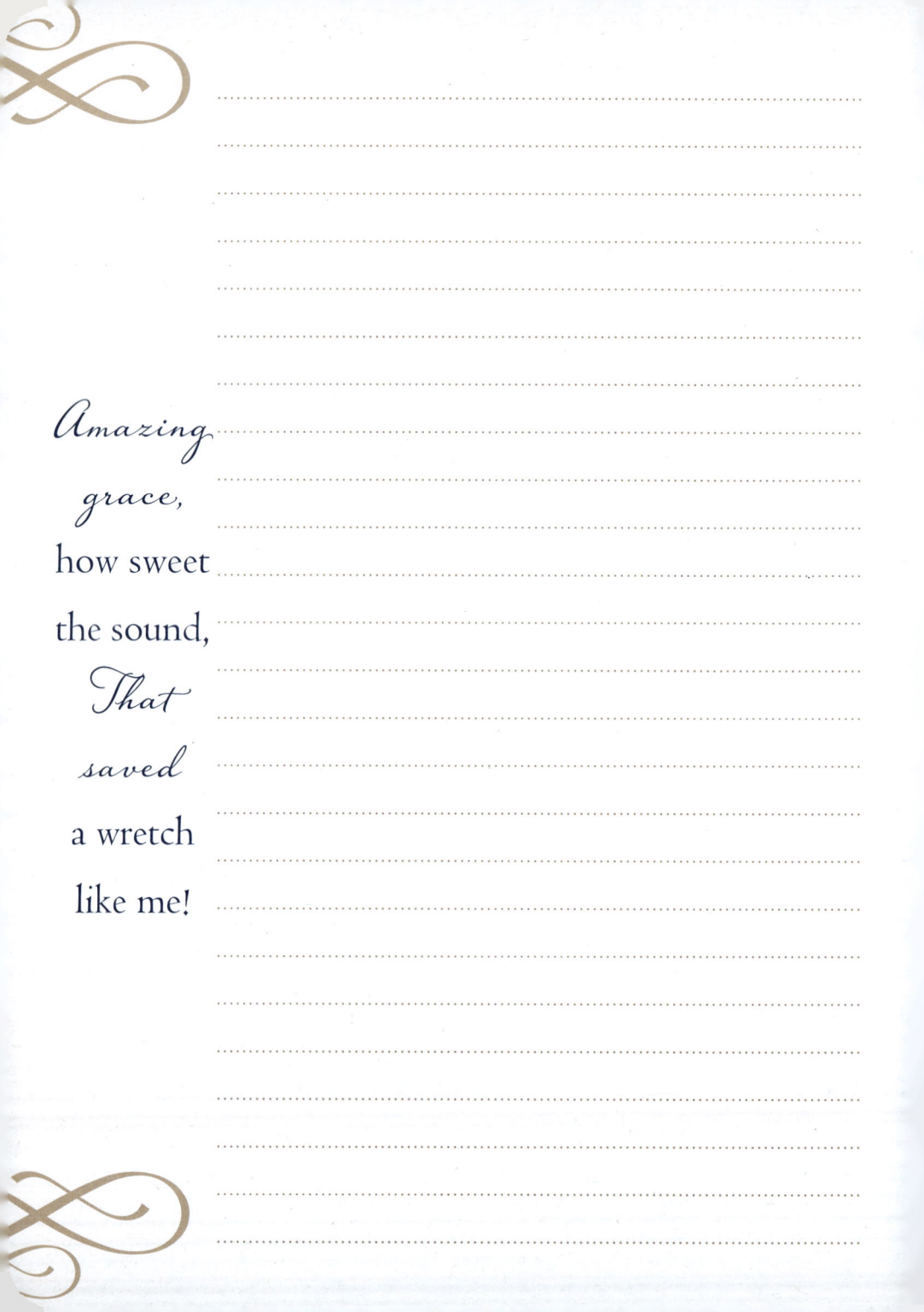

Amazing grace, how sweet the sound, That saved a wretch like me!

I once *was lost* but now am found, *Was blind* but now I see.

'Twas grace that taught my heart to fear, And grace my fears relieved;

How *precious* did that *grace* appear The hour *I first believed!*

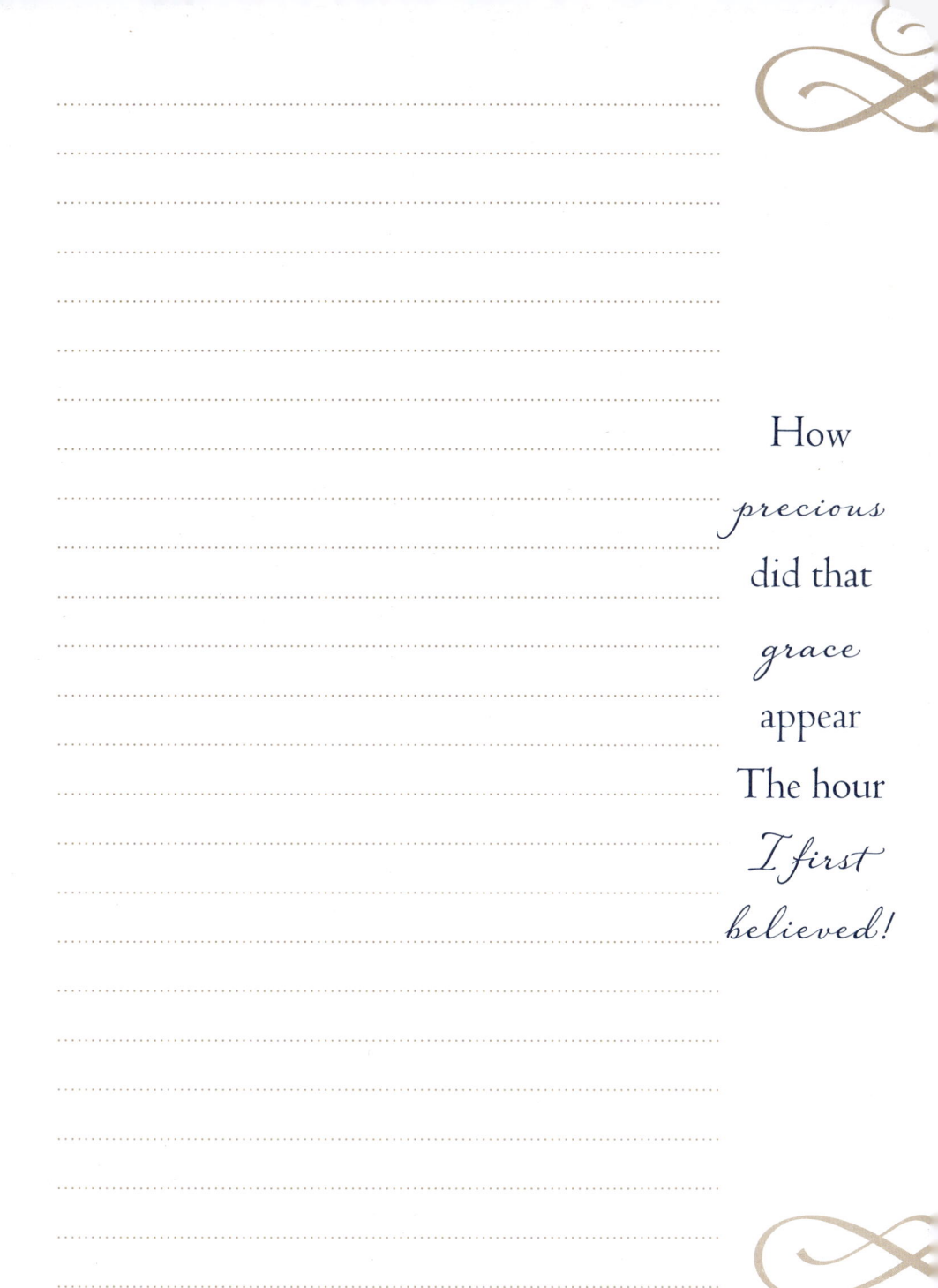

Through many dangers, toils, and snares, I have already come;

'Twas *grace* that brought me safe thus far, *And grace* will lead me home.

The Lord has promised good to me. His Word my hope secures.

He will my shield and portion be, As long as life endures.

The earth shall soon dissolve like snow, The sun forbear to shine;

But God, who called me here below, Will be forever mine.

When
we've been
there ten
thousand
years,
*Bright
shining*
as the sun;

We've no less days *to sing God's praise* Than when we'd first begun.

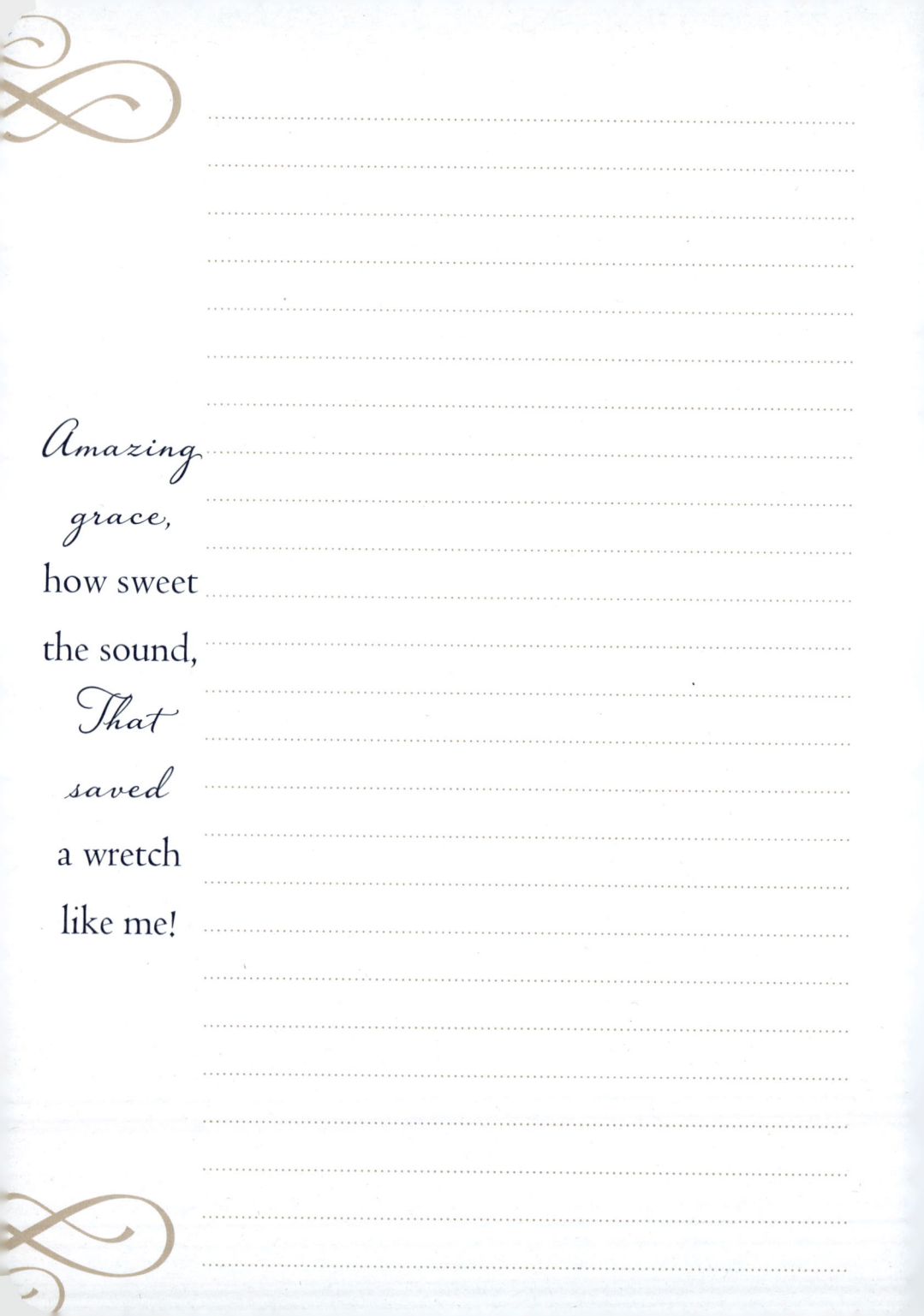

Amazing grace, how sweet the sound, That saved a wretch like me!

I once *was lost* but now am found, *Was blind* but now I see.

> 'Twas grace that taught my heart to fear, And grace my fears relieved;

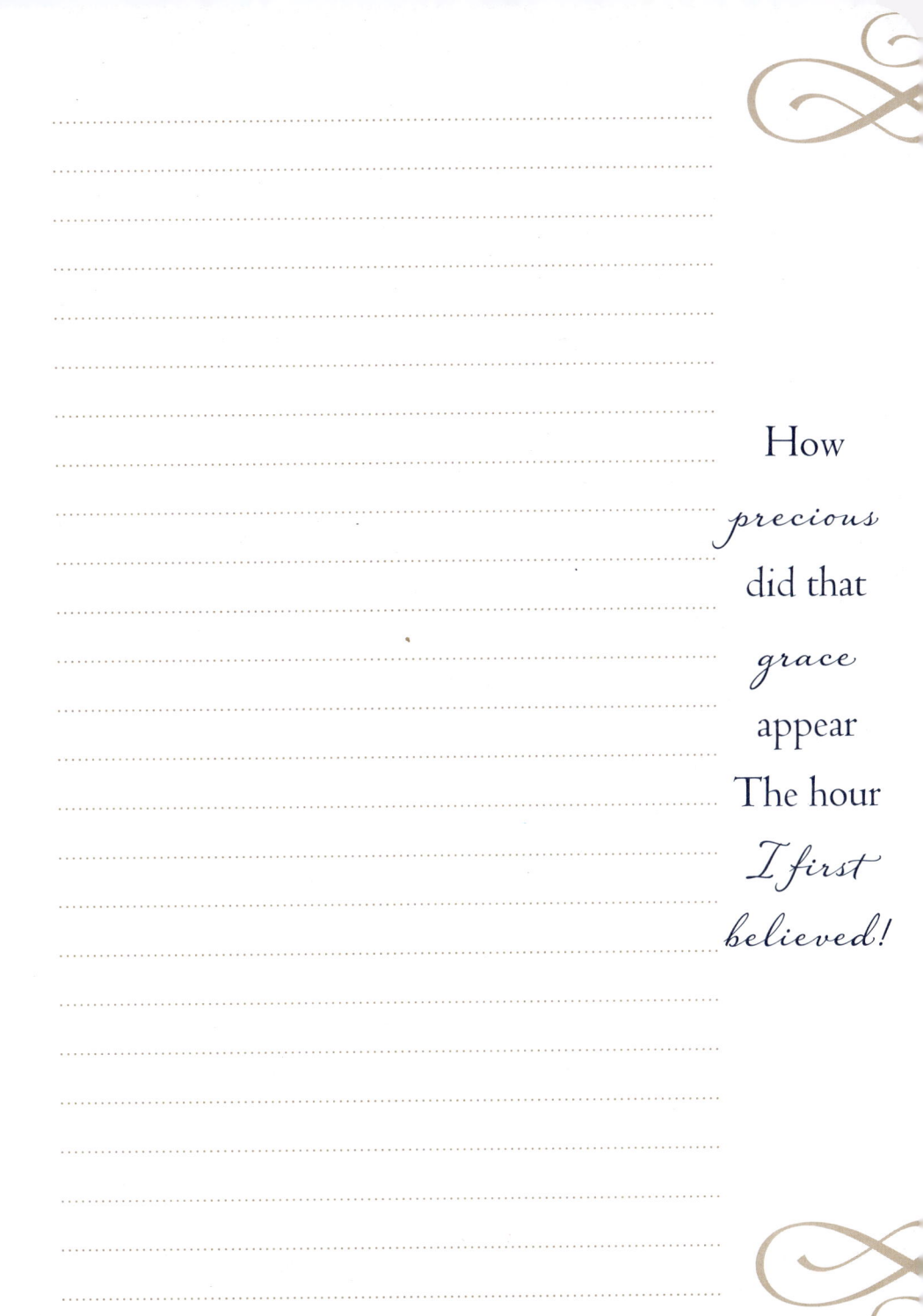

How *precious* did that *grace* appear The hour *I first believed!*

Through many dangers, toils, and snares, I have already come;

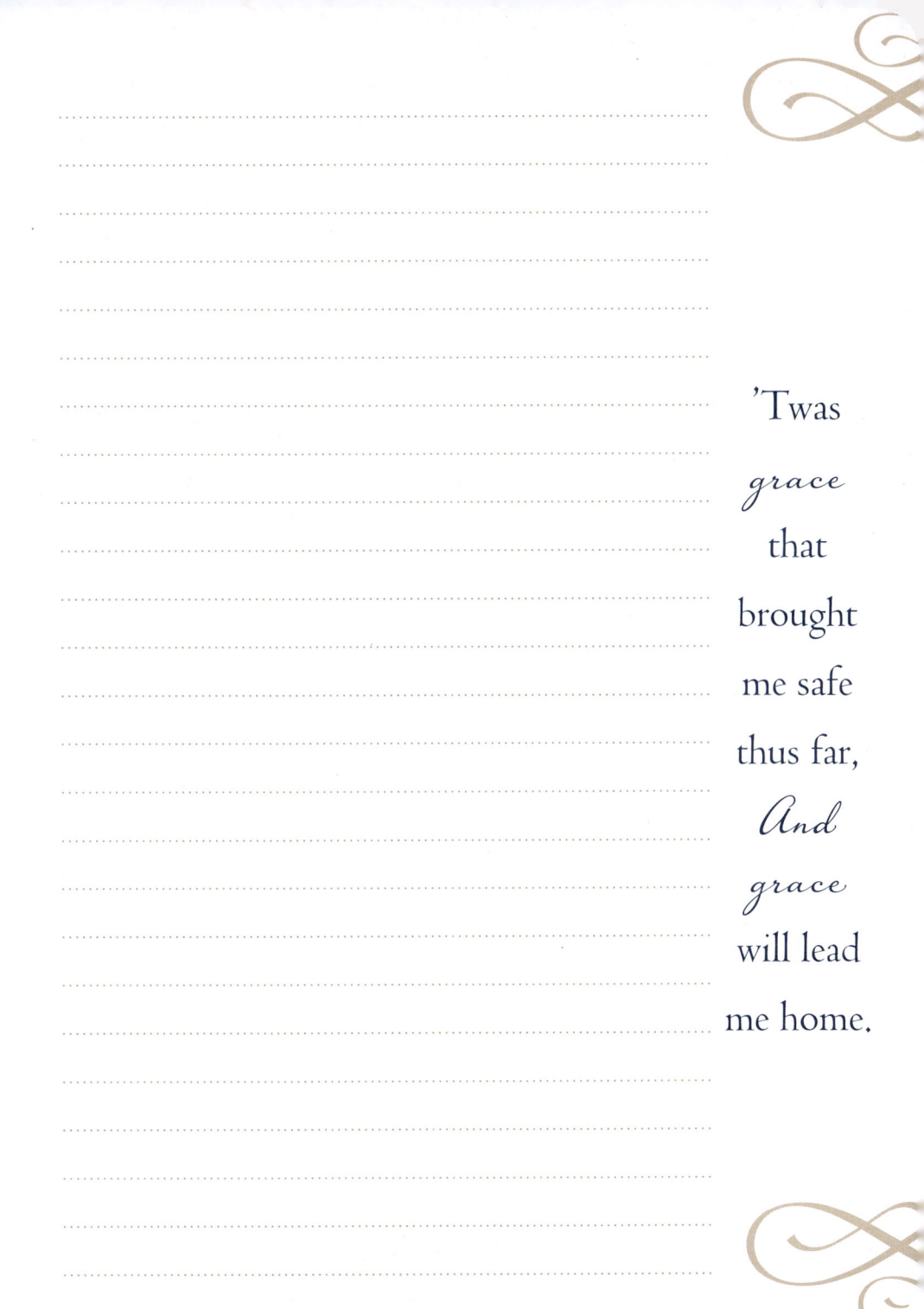

'Twas *grace* that brought me safe thus far, *And grace* will lead me home.

The Lord has promised good to me. His Word my hope secures.

He will my shield and portion be, As long as life endures.

The earth
shall soon
dissolve
like snow,
The sun
forbear
to shine;

But God, who called me here below, Will be forever mine.

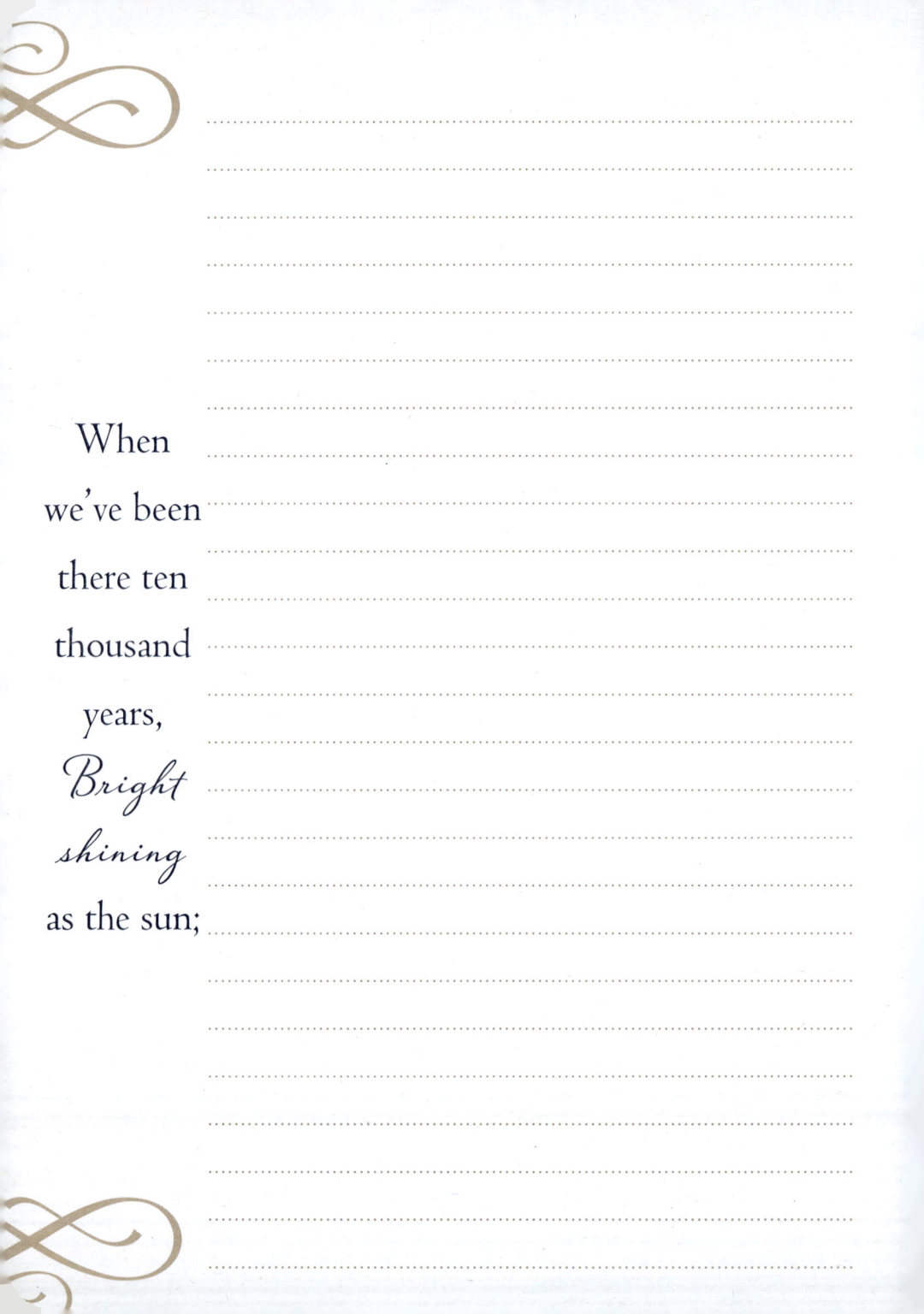

When
we've been
there ten
thousand
years,
Bright
shining
as the sun;

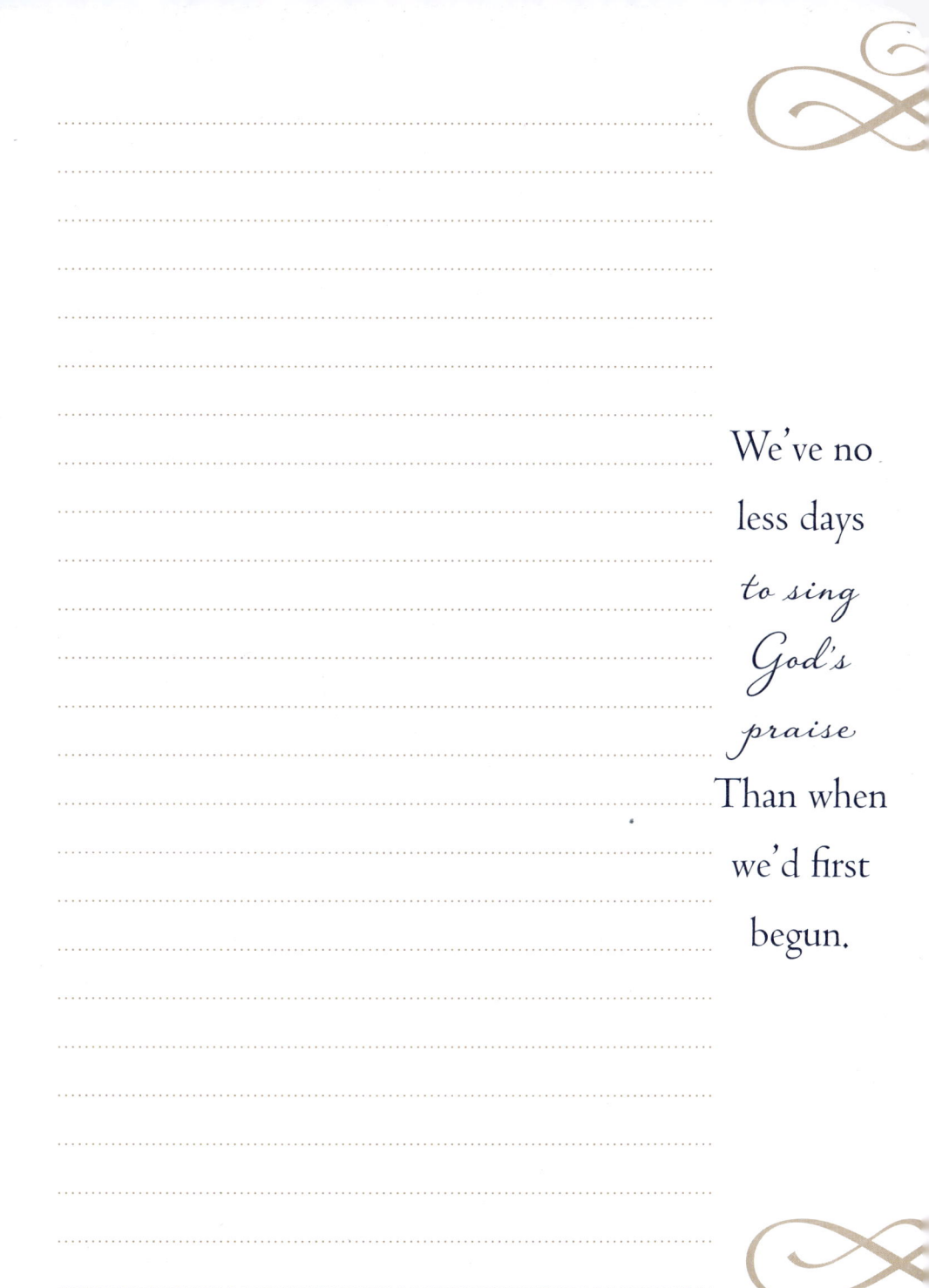

We've no less days to sing God's praise Than when we'd first begun.

Amazing grace, how sweet the sound, That saved a wretch like me!

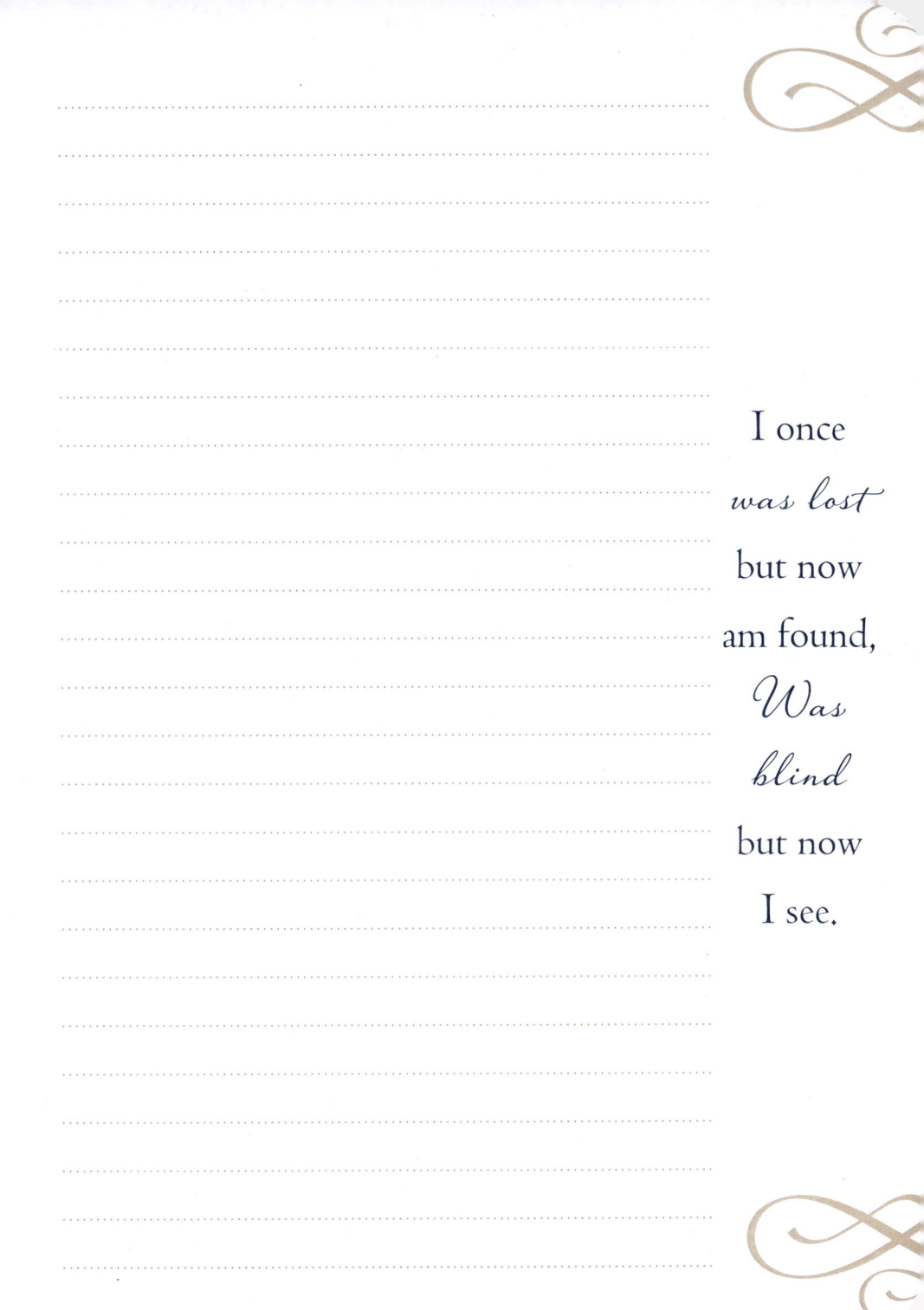

I once *was lost* but now am found, *Was blind* but now I see.

'Twas grace that taught my heart to fear, And grace my fears relieved;

How *precious* did that *grace* appear
The hour *I first* believed!

Through many dangers, toils, and snares, I have already come;

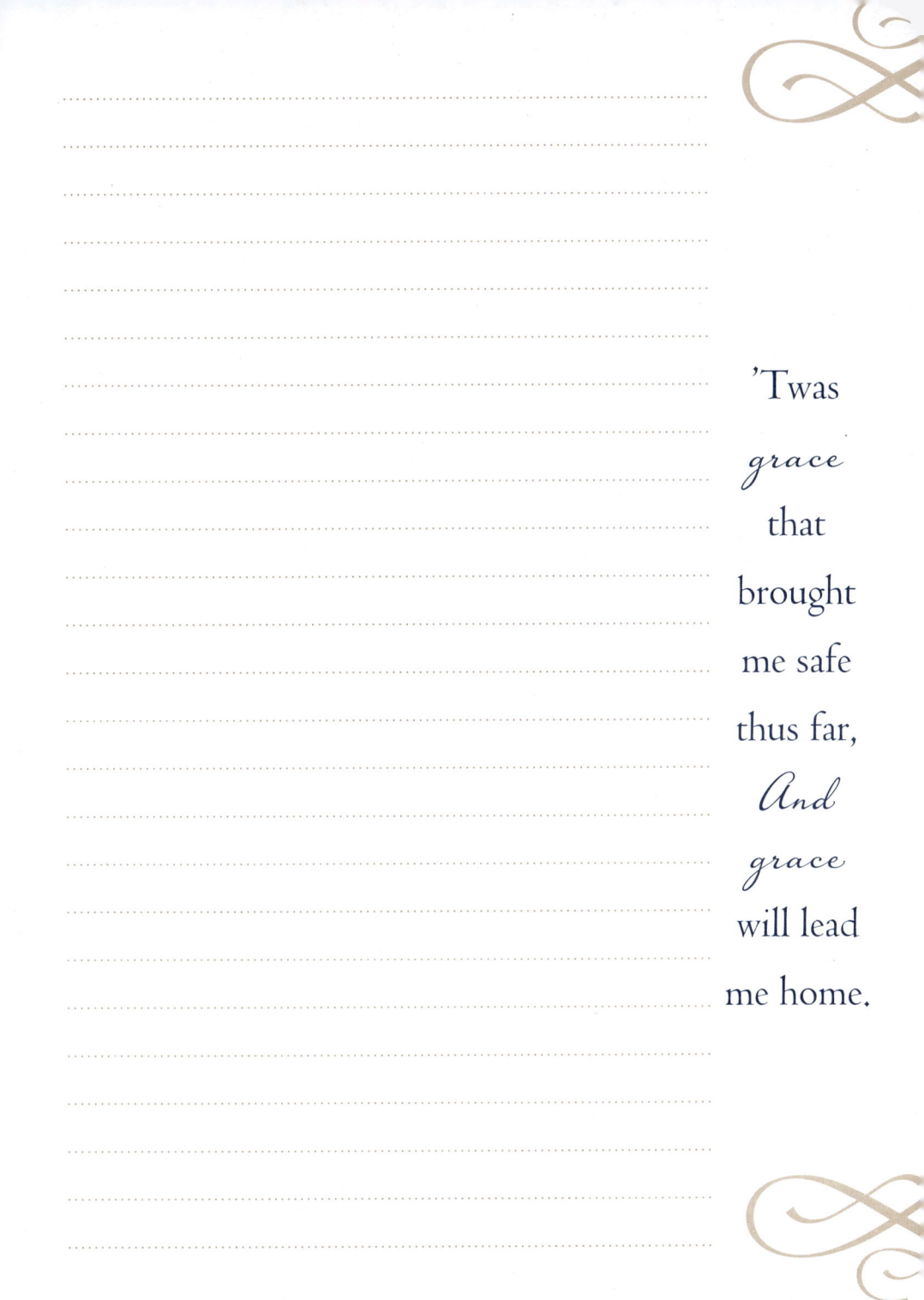

'Twas *grace* that brought me safe thus far, *And grace* will lead me home.

The Lord has promised good to me. His Word my hope secures.

He will my shield and portion be, As long as life endures.

The earth shall soon dissolve like snow, The sun forbear to shine;

But God, who called me here below, Will be forever mine.

When
we've been
there ten
thousand
years,
*Bright
shining*
as the sun;

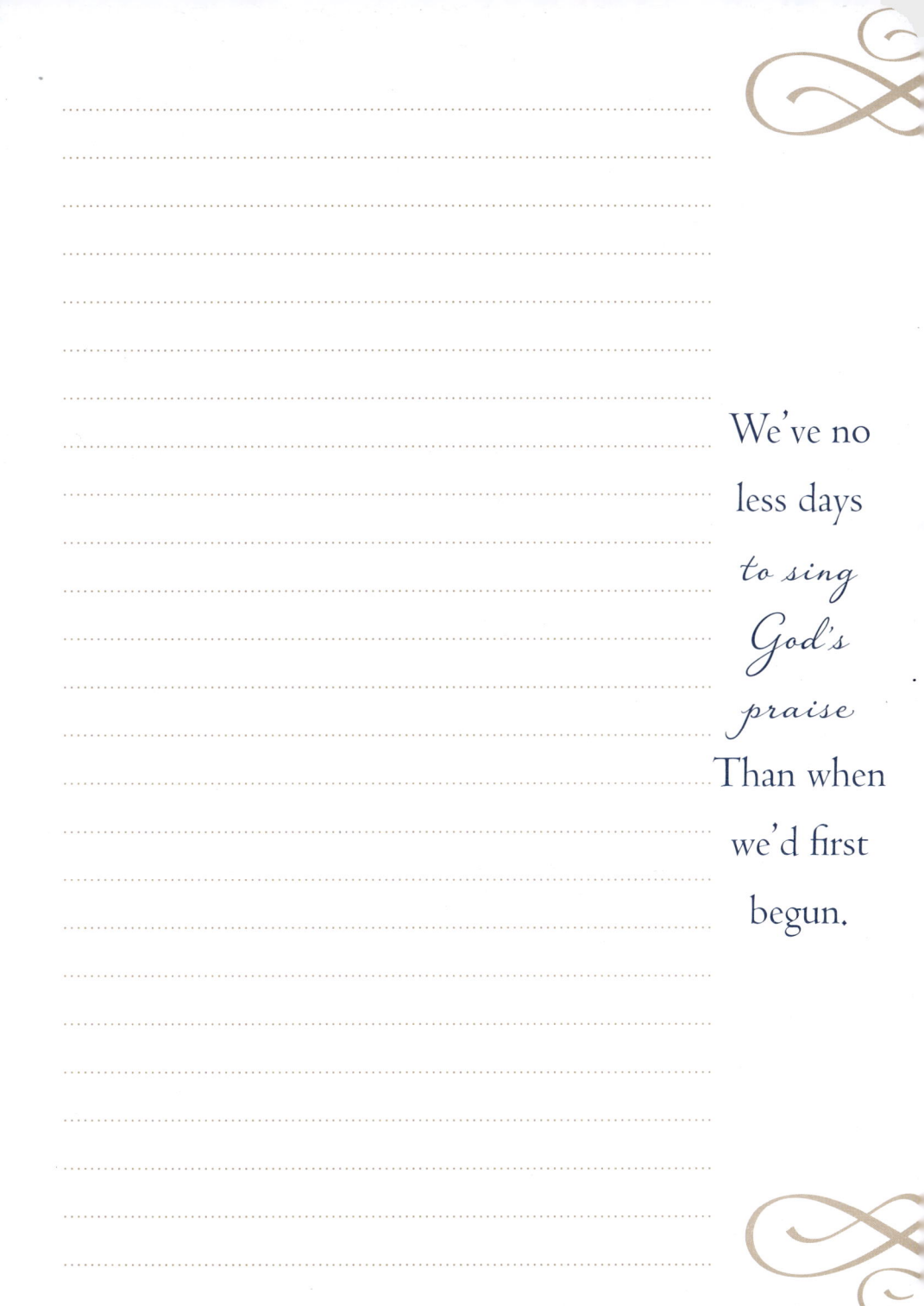

> We've no less days *to sing God's praise* Than when we'd first begun.

Amazing grace, how sweet the sound, That saved a wretch like me!

I once was lost but now am found, *Was blind* but now I see.

> 'Twas grace that taught my heart to fear, And grace my fears relieved;

How precious did that grace appear The hour I first believed!

Through many dangers, *toils, and snares,* I have already come;

'Twas grace that brought me safe thus far, And grace will lead me home.

The Lord has promised good to me. His Word my hope secures.

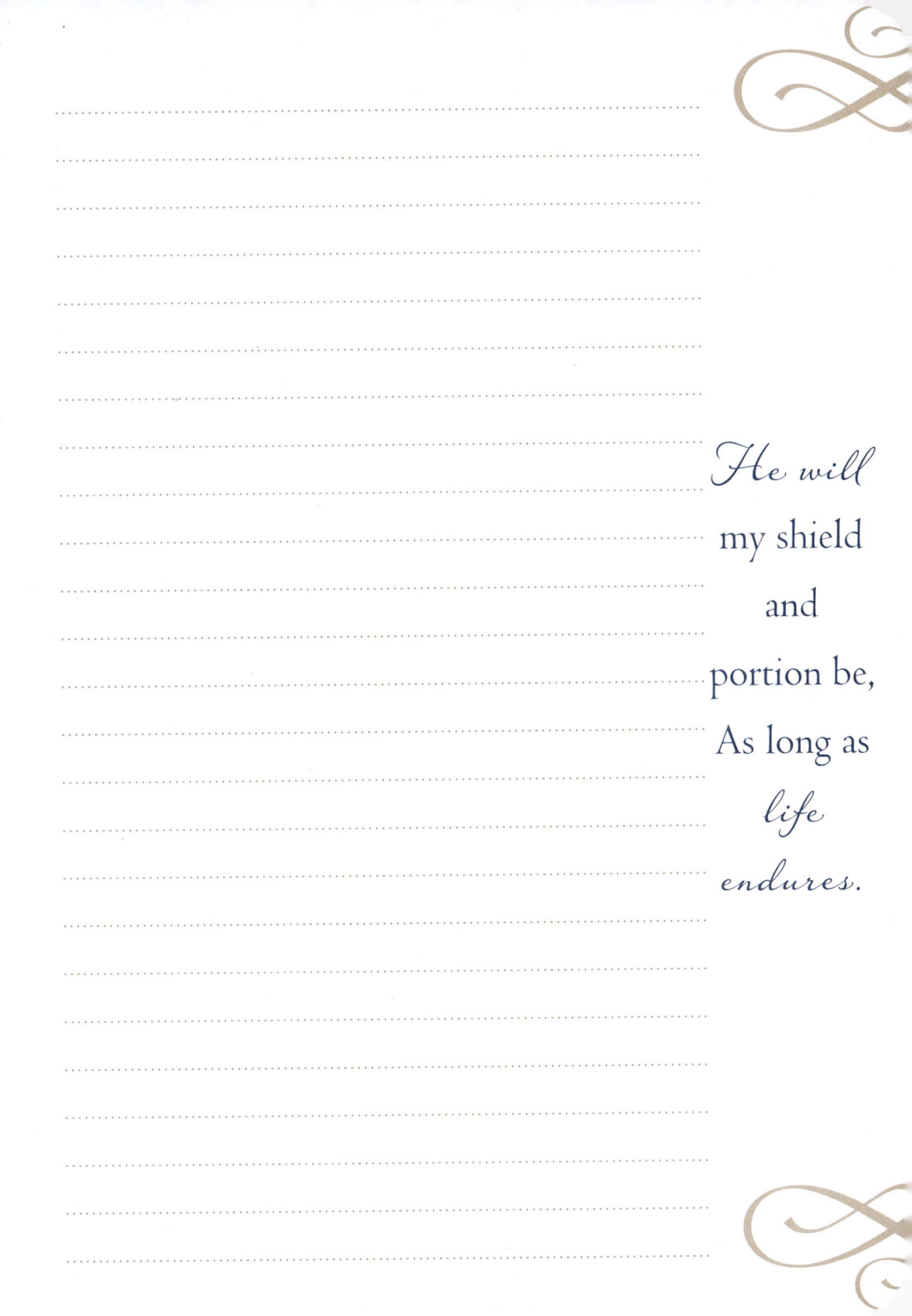

He will my shield and portion be, As long as life endures.

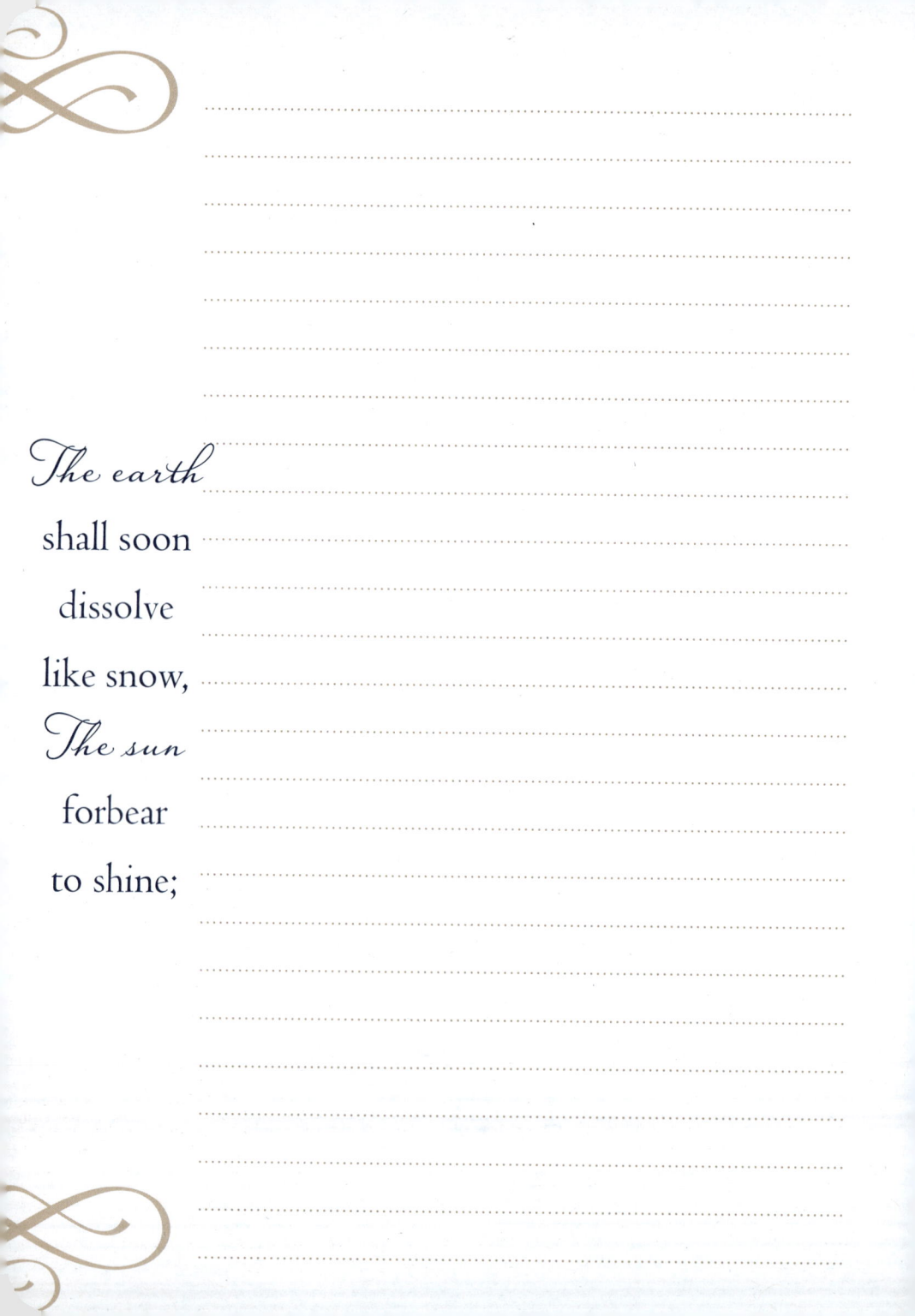

The earth shall soon dissolve like snow, The sun forbear to shine;

*But God,
who called
me here
below,
Will be
forever
mine.*

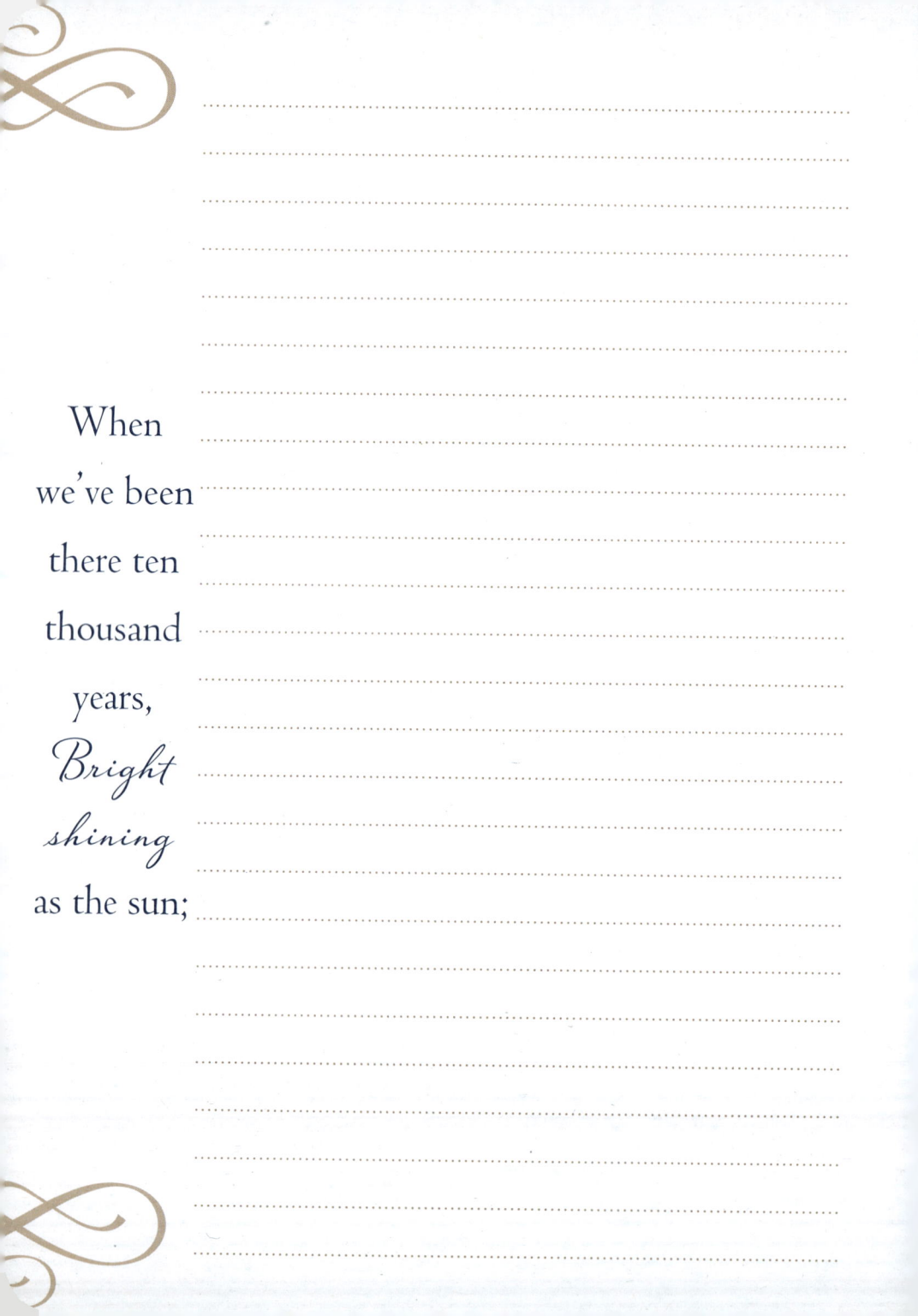

When
we've been
there ten
thousand
years,
*Bright
shining*
as the sun;

We've no less days to sing God's praise Than when we'd first begun.

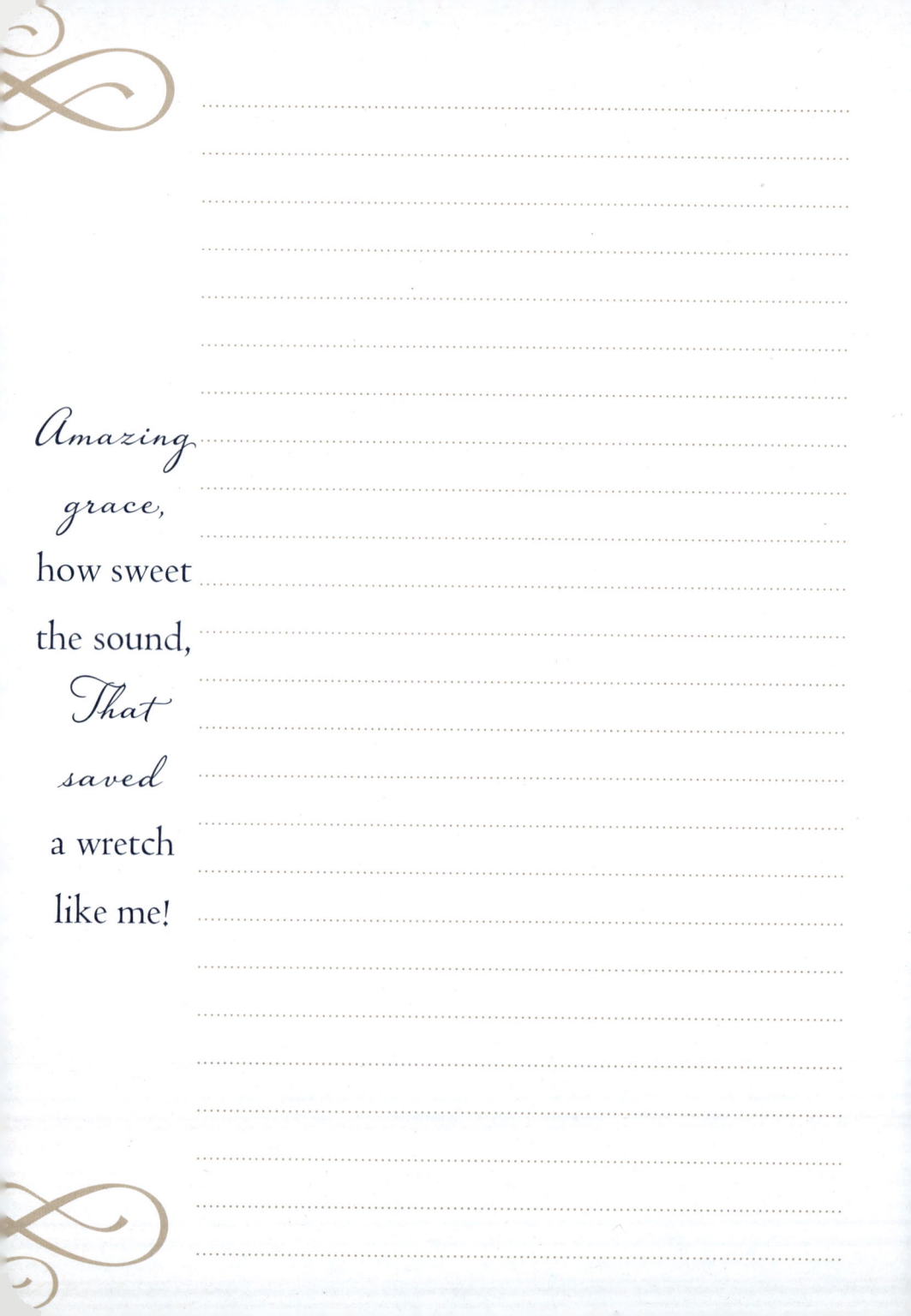

Amazing grace, how sweet the sound, That saved a wretch like me!

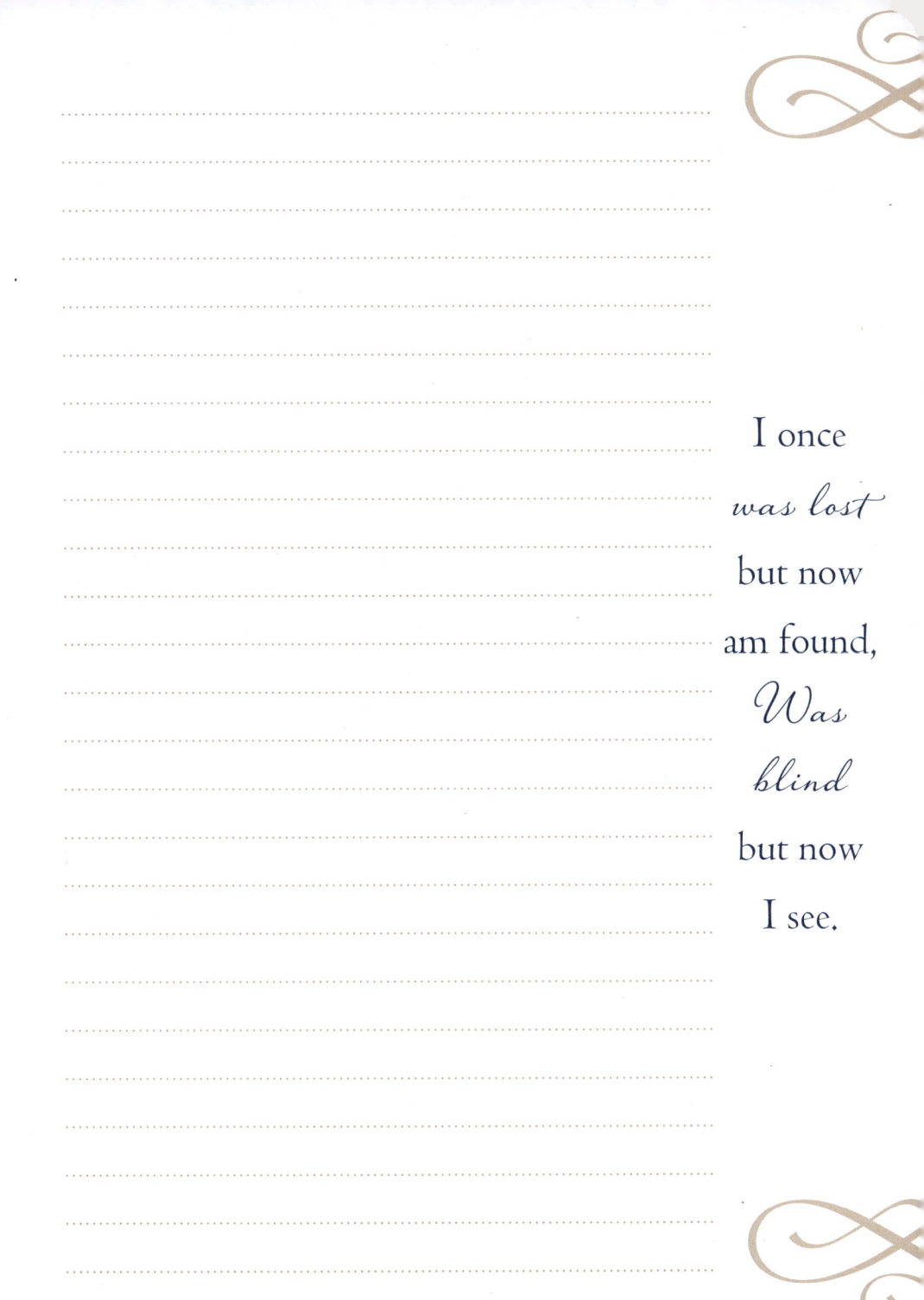

I once *was lost* but now am found, *Was blind* but now I see.

'Twas grace that taught my heart to fear, And grace my fears relieved;

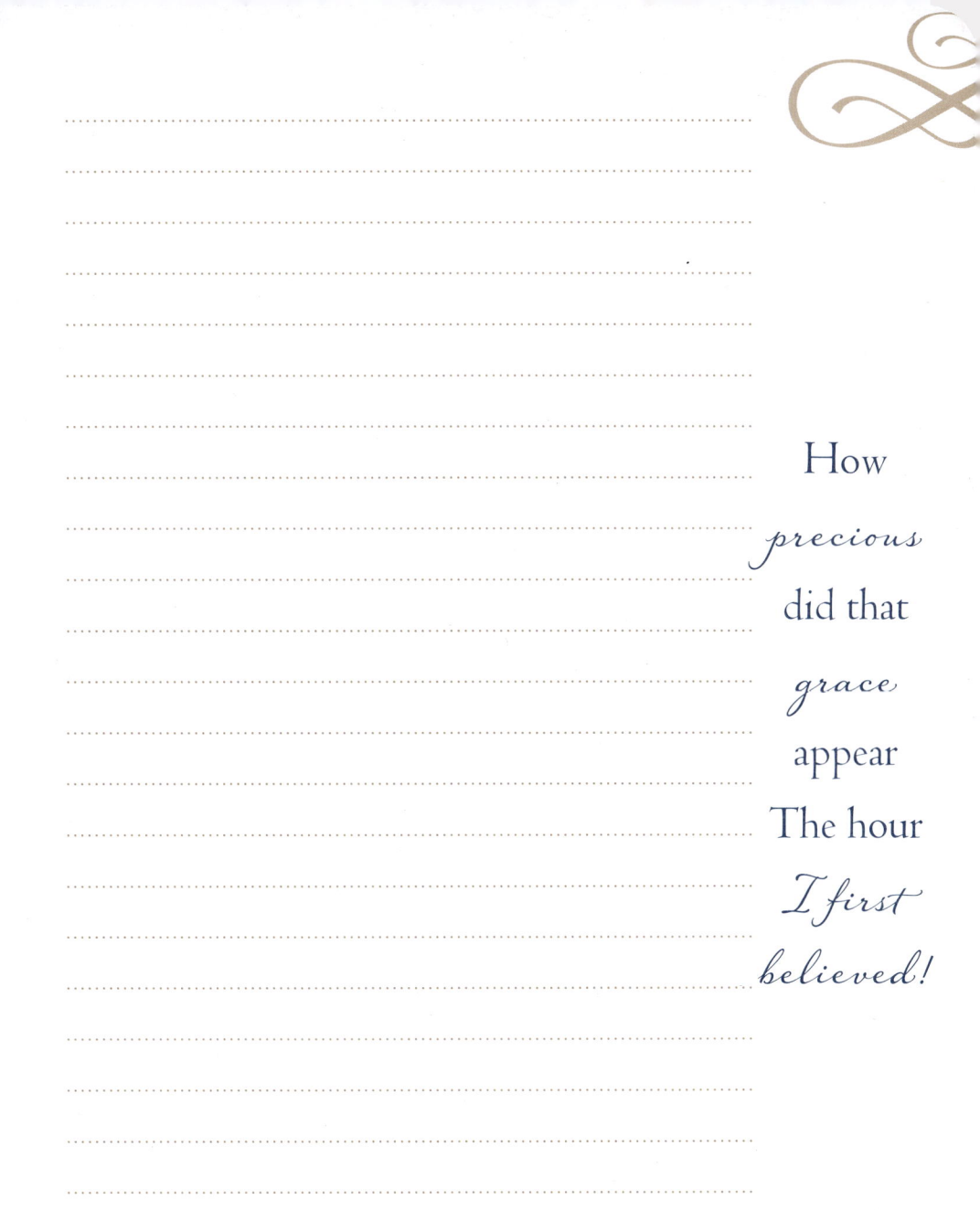

How *precious* did that *grace* appear
The hour *I first believed!*

Through many dangers, toils, and snares, I have already come;

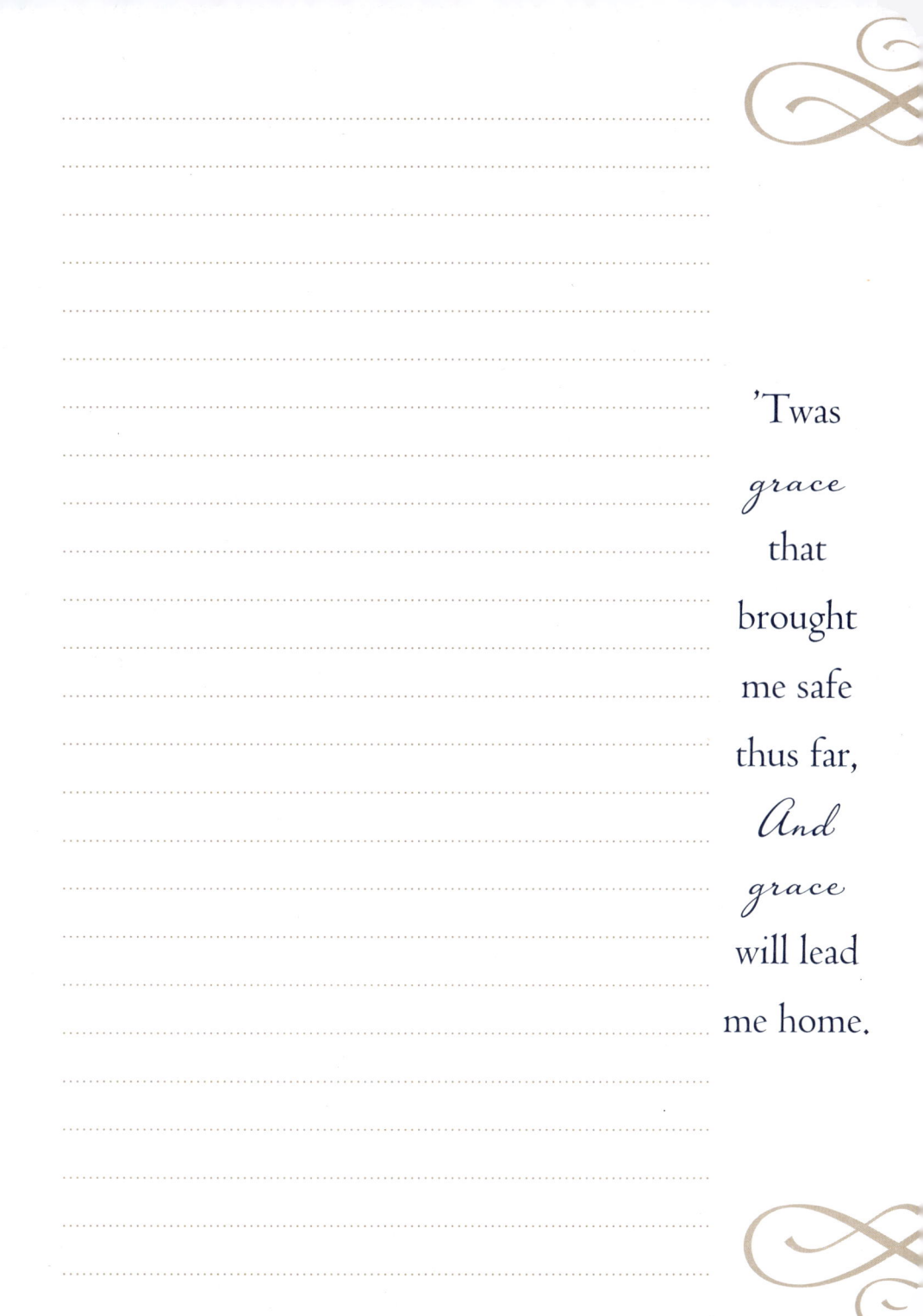

'Twas *grace* that brought me safe thus far, *And grace* will lead me home.

The Lord has promised good to me. His Word my hope secures.

He will my shield and portion be, As long as life endures.

The earth shall soon dissolve like snow, The sun forbear to shine;

But God, who called me here below, Will be forever mine.

When
we've been
there ten
thousand
years,
*Bright
shining
as the sun;*

We've no less days to sing God's praise Than when we'd first begun.

Amazing grace, how sweet the sound, That saved a wretch like me!

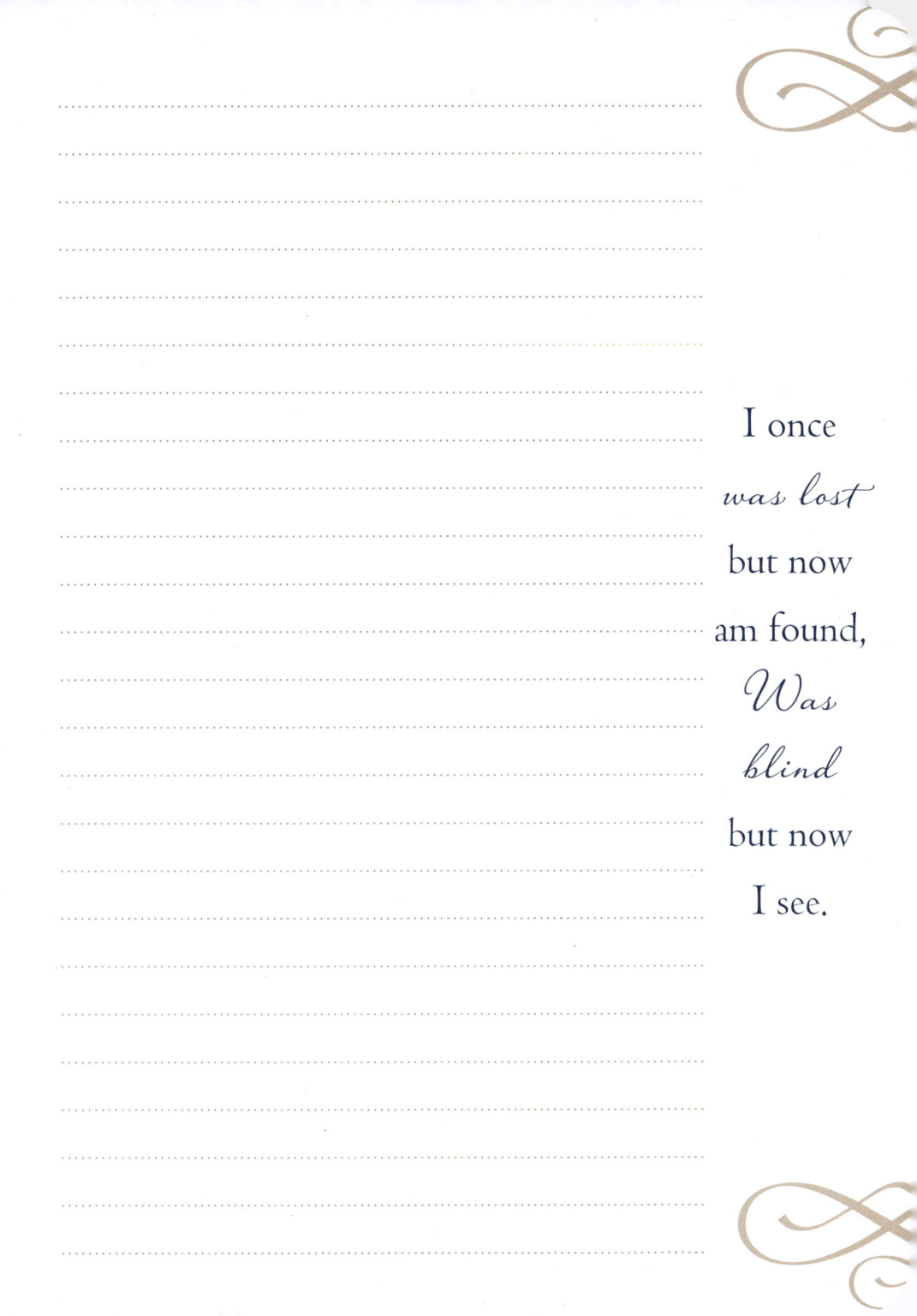

I once *was lost* but now am found, *Was blind* but now I see.

'Twas grace that taught my heart to fear, And grace my fears relieved;

How precious did that grace appear The hour I first believed!

Through many dangers, *toils, and snares,* I have already come;

'Twas *grace* that brought me safe thus far, *And grace* will lead me home.

The Lord has promised good to me. His Word my hope secures.

He will my shield and portion be, As long as life endures.

The earth shall soon dissolve like snow, The sun forbear to shine;

But God, who called me here below, Will be forever mine.

When we've been there ten thousand years, *Bright shining* as the sun;

We've no less days *to sing God's praise* Than when we'd first begun.

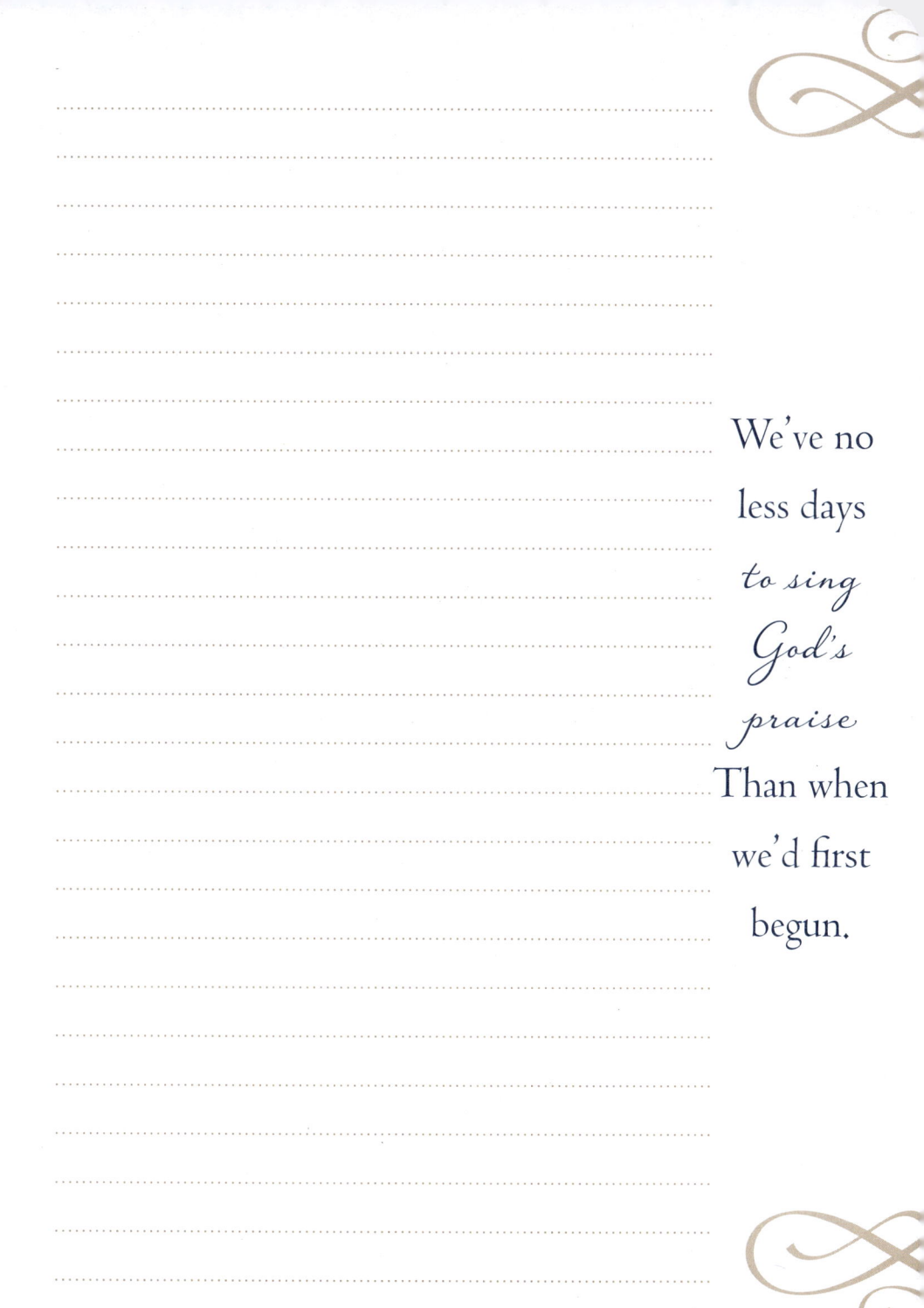

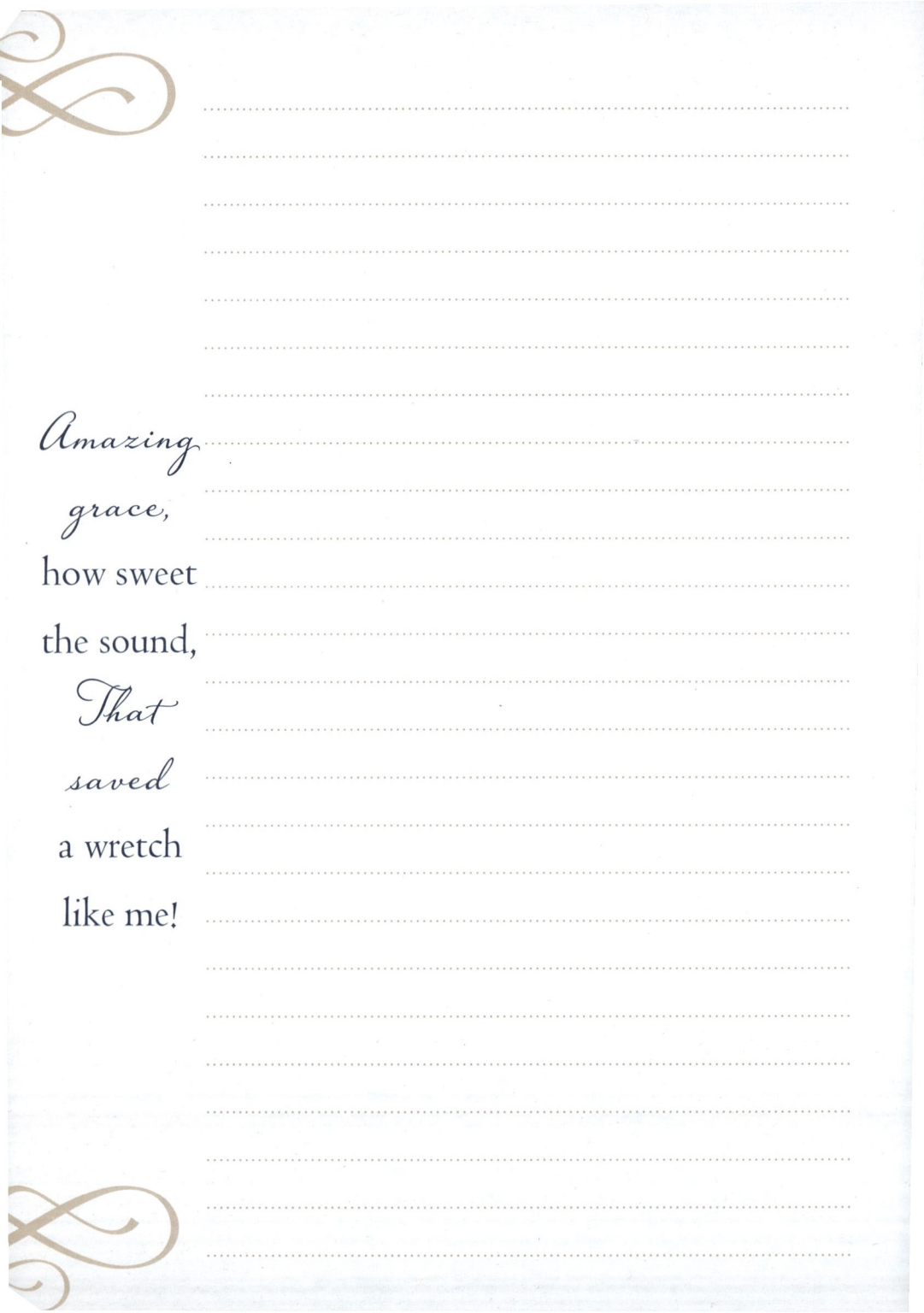

Amazing grace, how sweet the sound, That saved a wretch like me!

I once *was lost* but now am found, *Was blind* but now I see.

> 'Twas grace that taught my heart to fear, And grace my fears relieved;

How *precious* did that *grace* appear The hour *I first believed!*

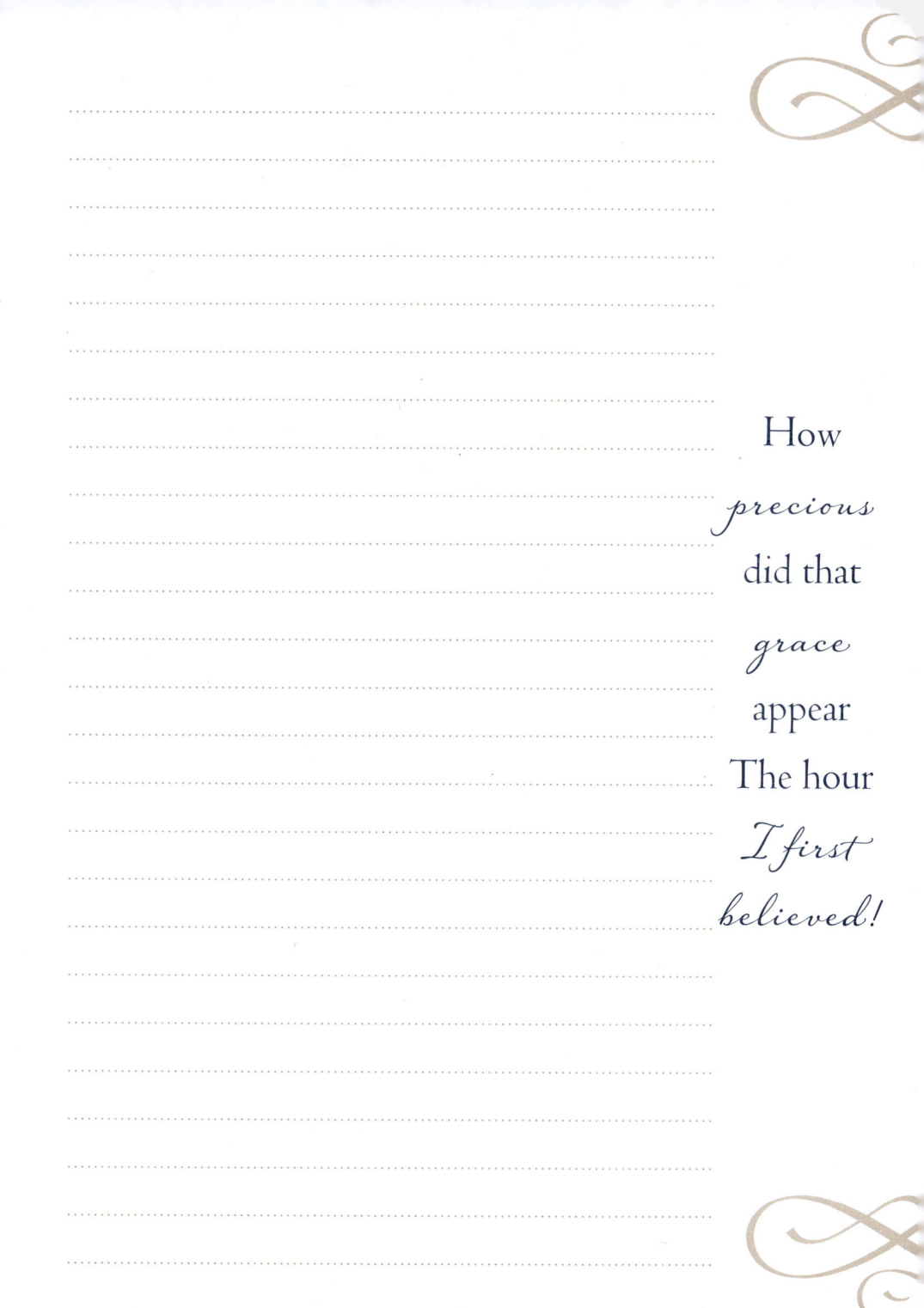

> Through many dangers, toils, and snares, I have already come;

'Twas grace that brought me safe thus far, And grace will lead me home.

The Lord has promised good to me. His Word my hope secures.

He will my shield and portion be, As long as life endures.

The earth
shall soon
dissolve
like snow,
The sun
forbear
to shine;

*But God,
who called
me here
below,
Will be
forever
mine.*

When we've been there ten thousand years,
Bright shining as the sun;

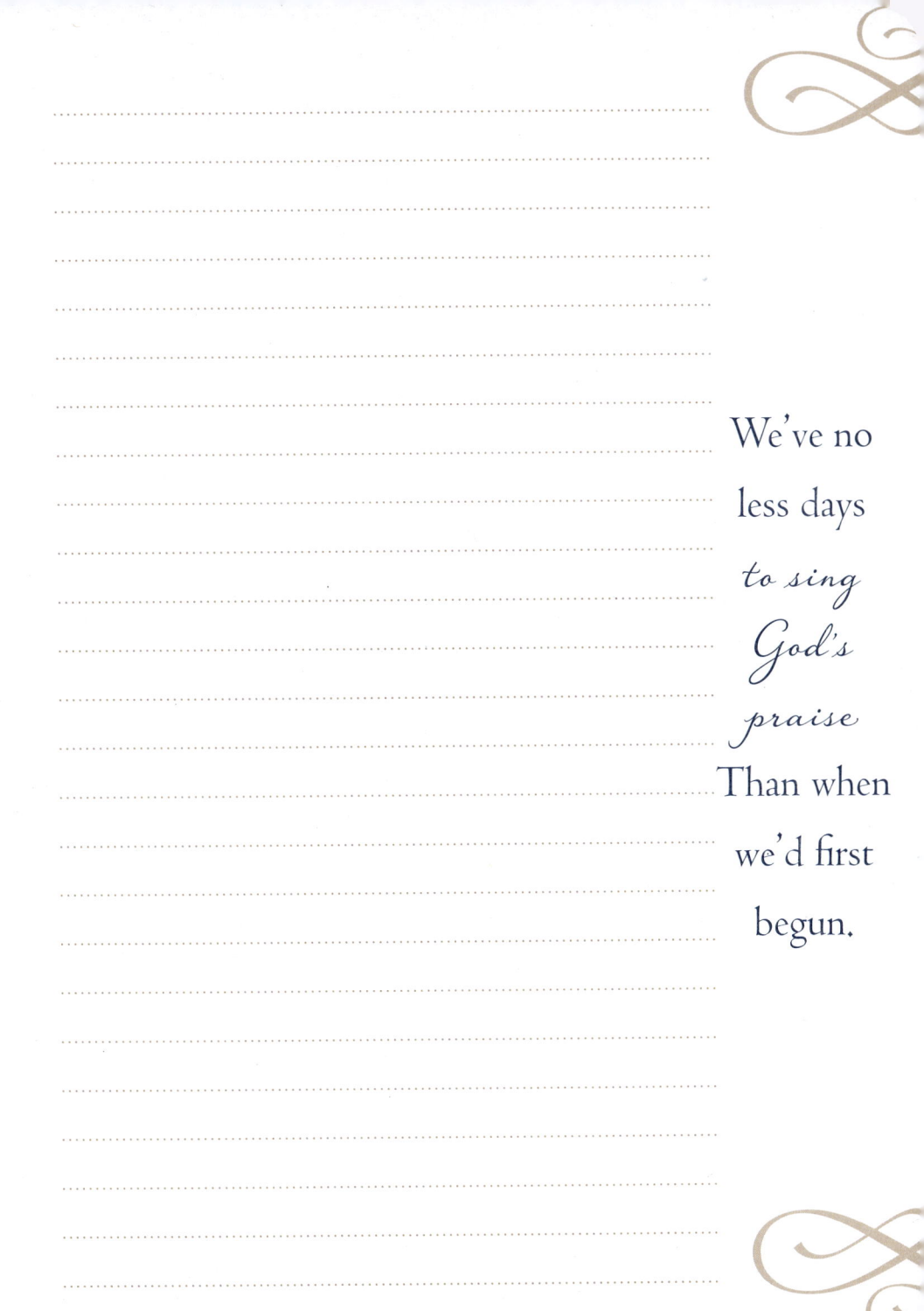

We've no less days *to sing God's praise* Than when we'd first begun.

Amazing grace, how sweet the sound, That saved a wretch like me!

I once *was lost* but now am found, *Was blind* but now I see.

'Twas grace that taught my heart to fear, And grace my fears relieved;

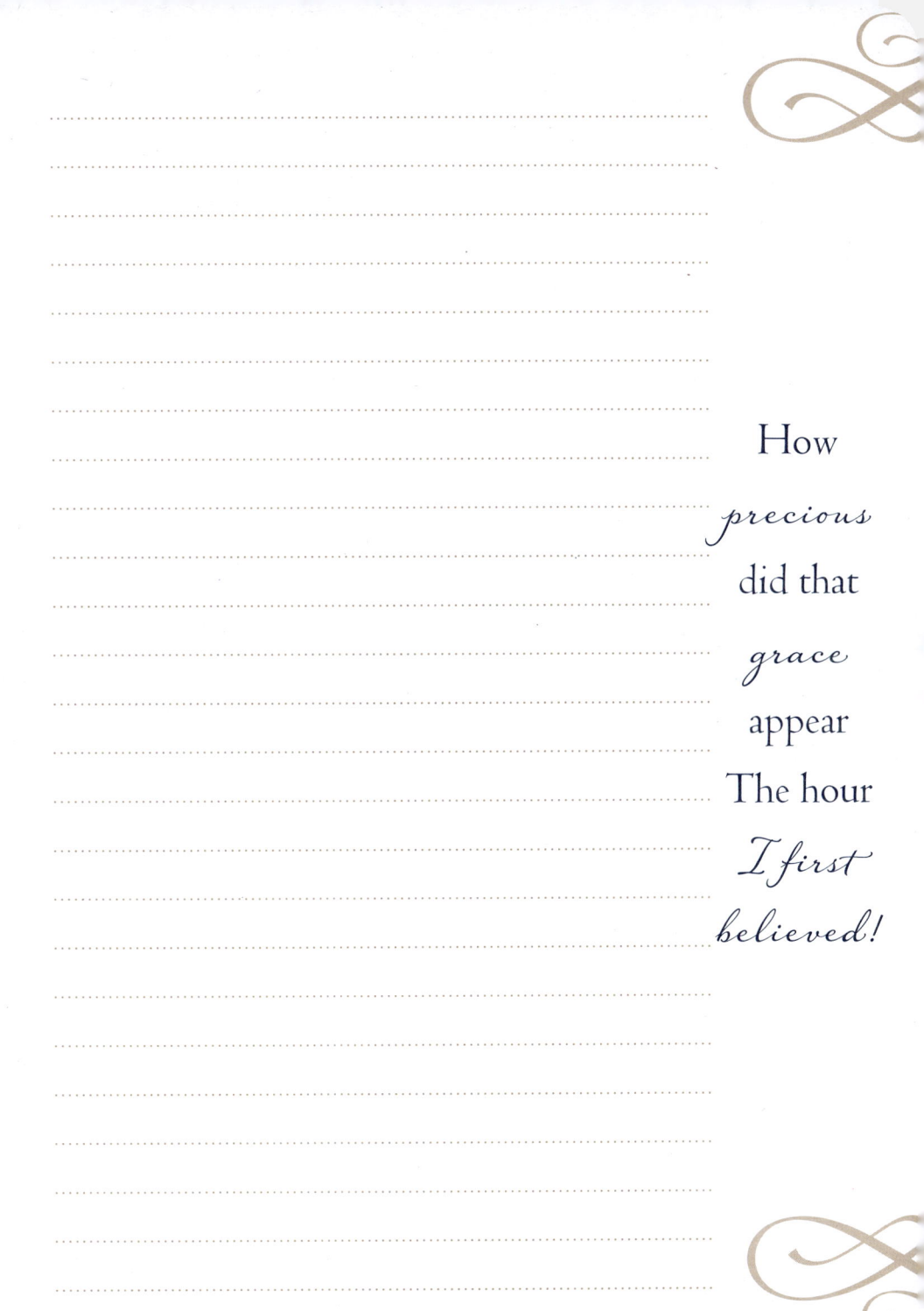

How precious did that grace appear The hour I first believed!

Through many dangers, toils, and snares, I have already come;

> 'Twas *grace* that brought me safe thus far, *And grace* will lead me home.

The Lord has promised good to me. His Word my hope secures.

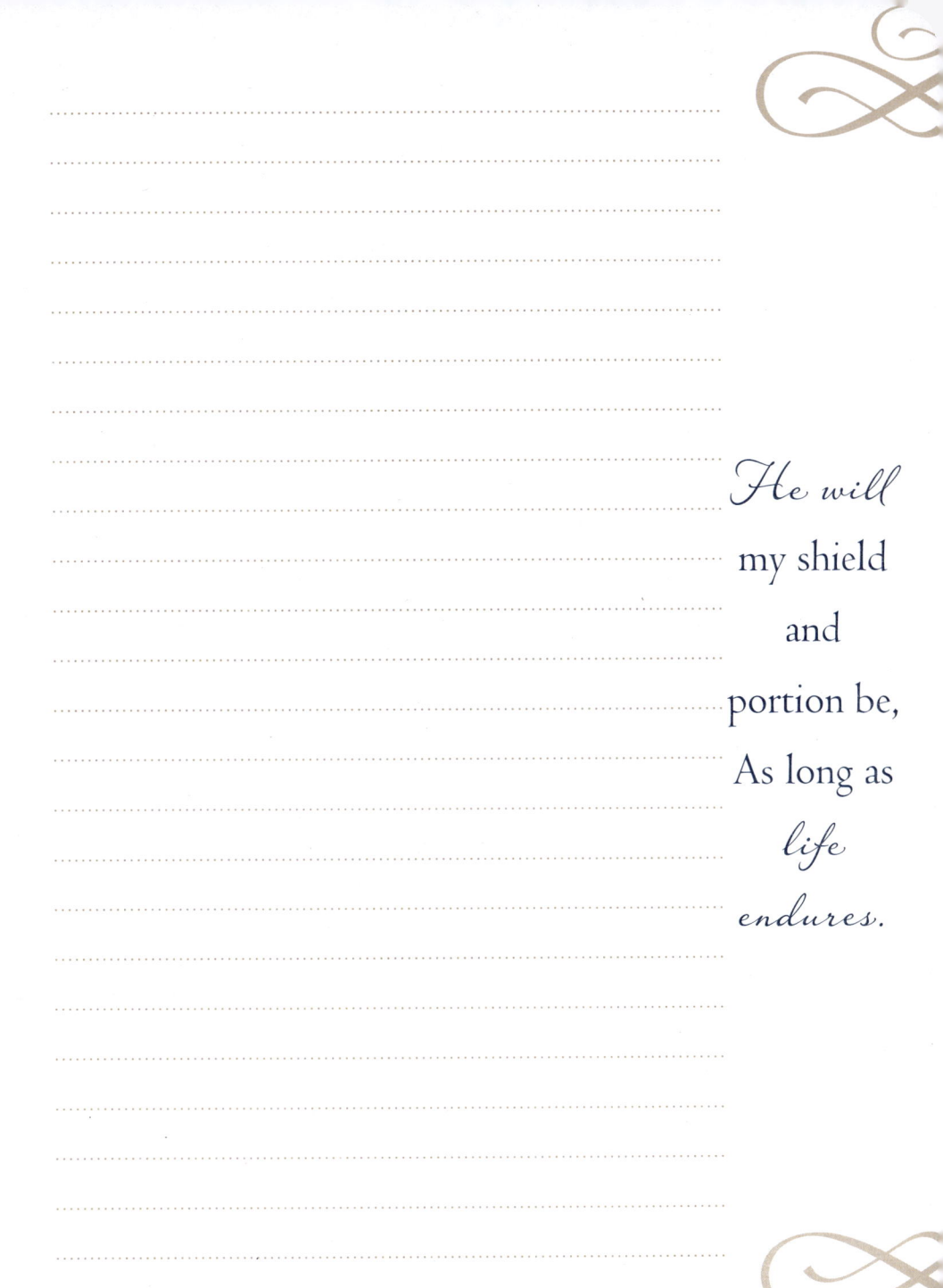

He will my shield and portion be, As long as life endures.

The earth
shall soon
dissolve
like snow,
The sun
forbear
to shine;

*But God,
who called
me here
below,
Will be
forever
mine.*

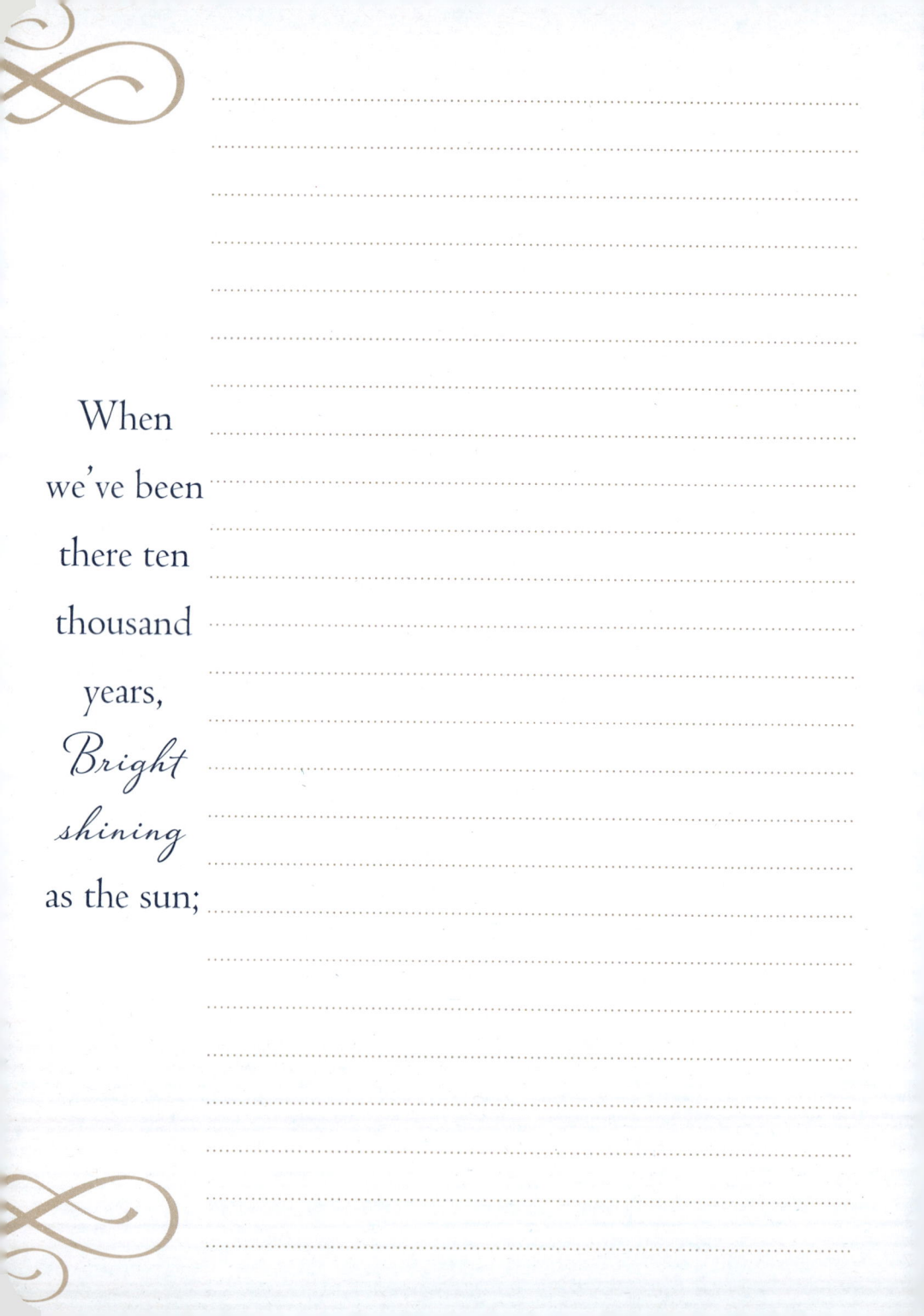

When
we've been
there ten
thousand
years,
*Bright
shining*
as the sun;

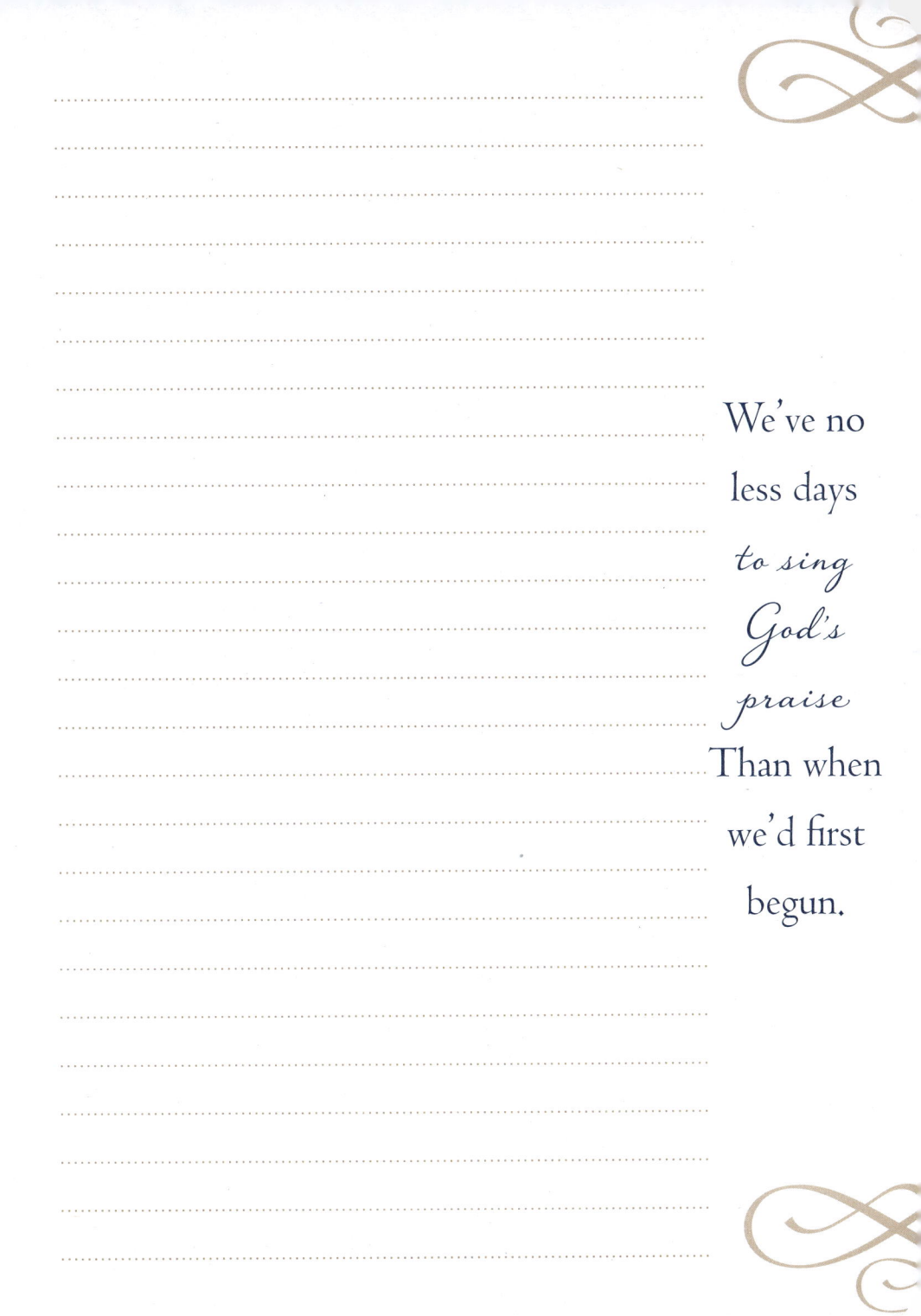

We've no less days *to sing God's praise* Than when we'd first begun.

Amazing grace, how sweet the sound, That saved a wretch like me!

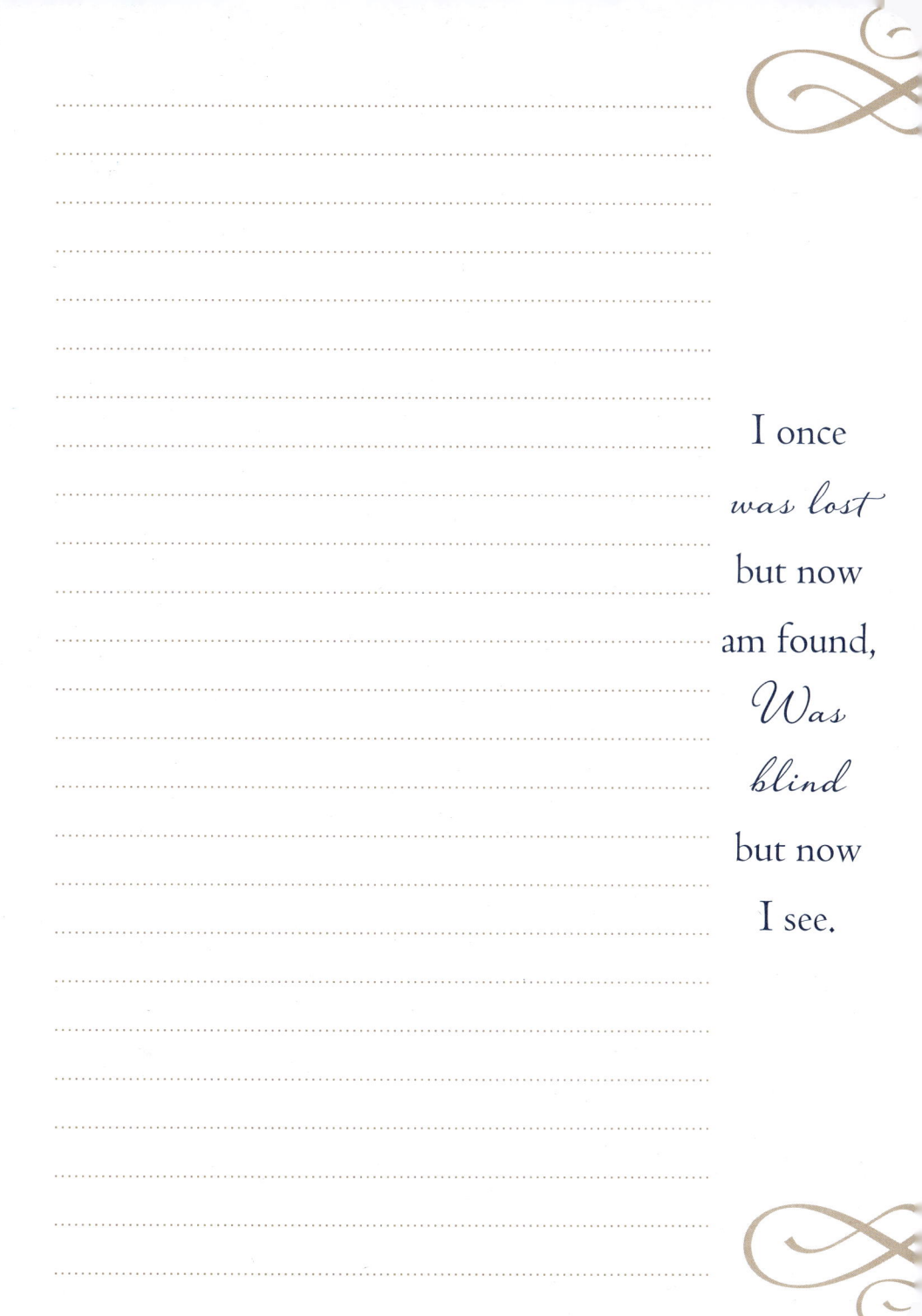

I once was lost but now am found, Was blind but now I see.

'Twas grace that taught my heart to fear, And grace my fears relieved;

How *precious* did that *grace* appear
The hour *I first believed!*

Through many dangers, *toils, and snares,* I have already come;

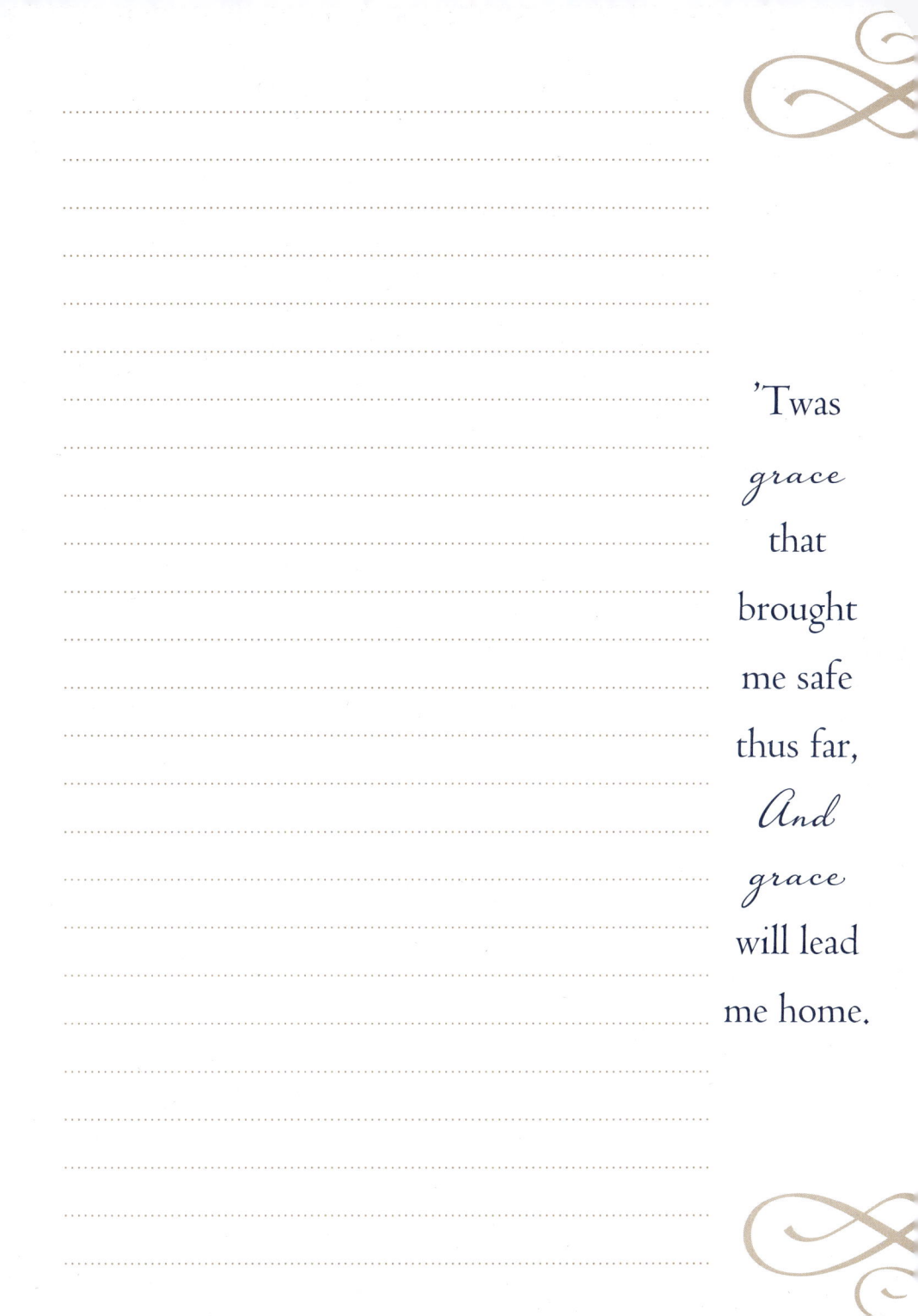

'Twas *grace* that brought me safe thus far, *And grace* will lead me home.

The Lord has promised good to me. His Word my hope secures.

> *He will my shield and portion be, As long as life endures.*

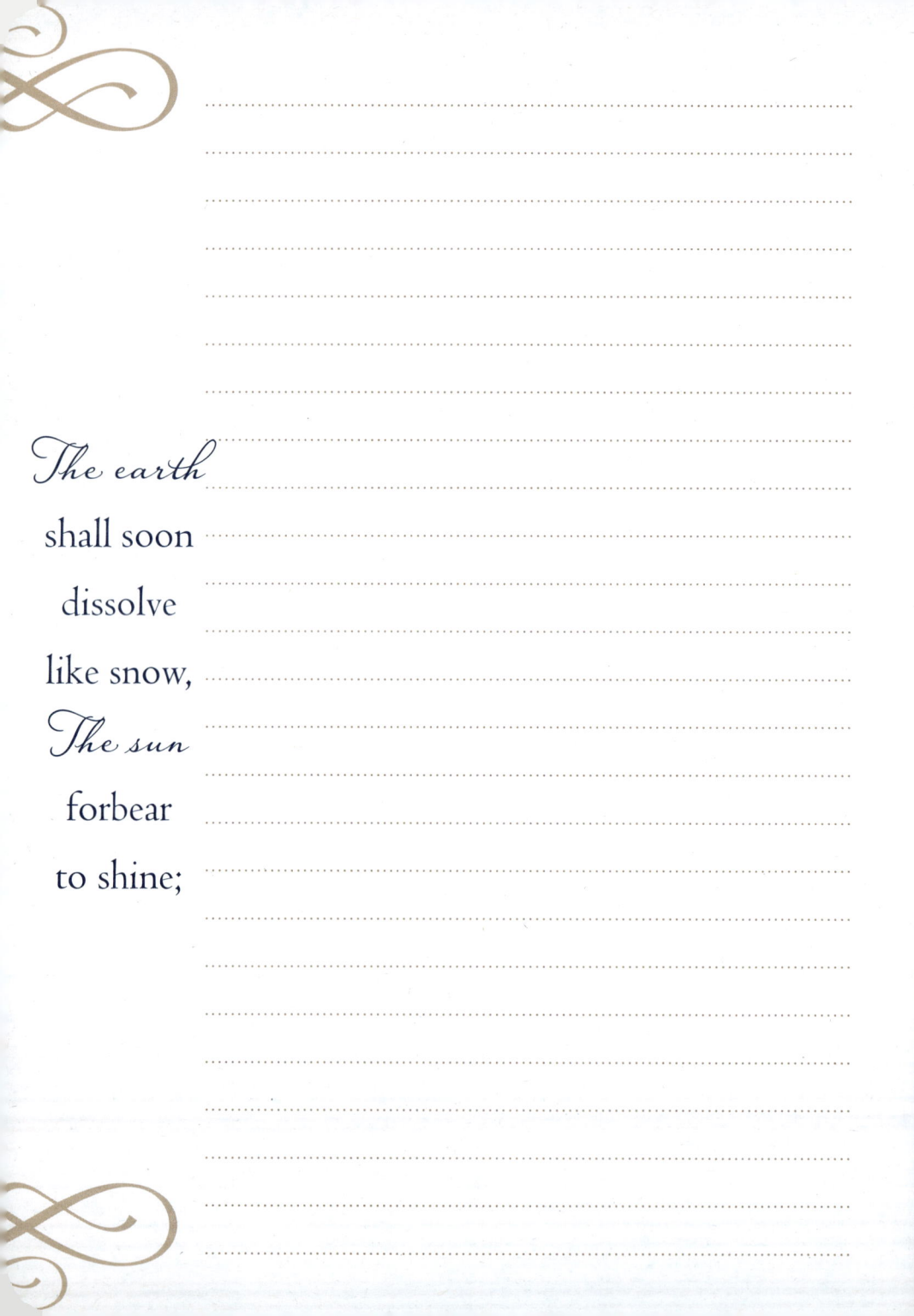

The earth shall soon dissolve like snow, The sun forbear to shine;

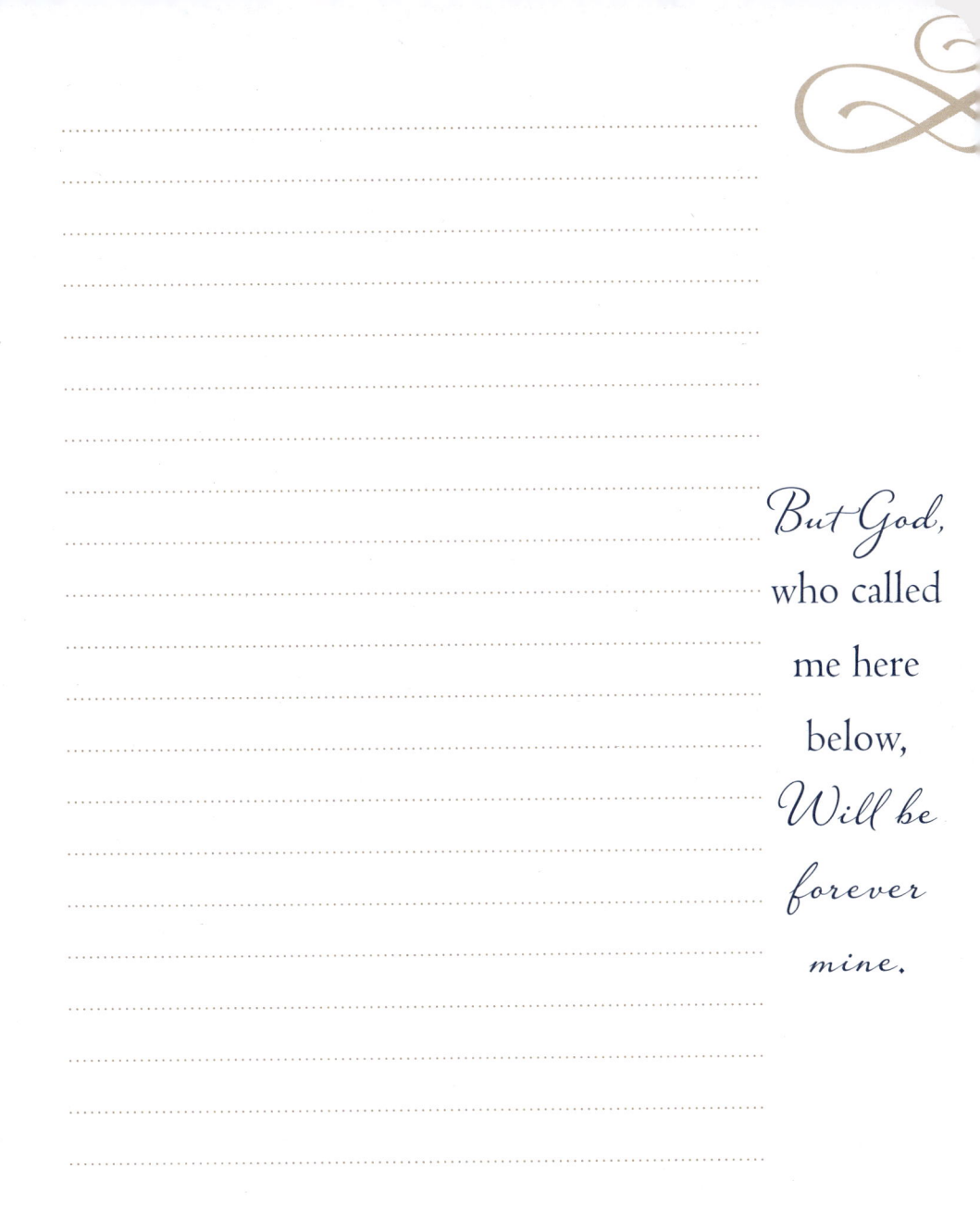

But God, who called me here below, Will be forever mine.

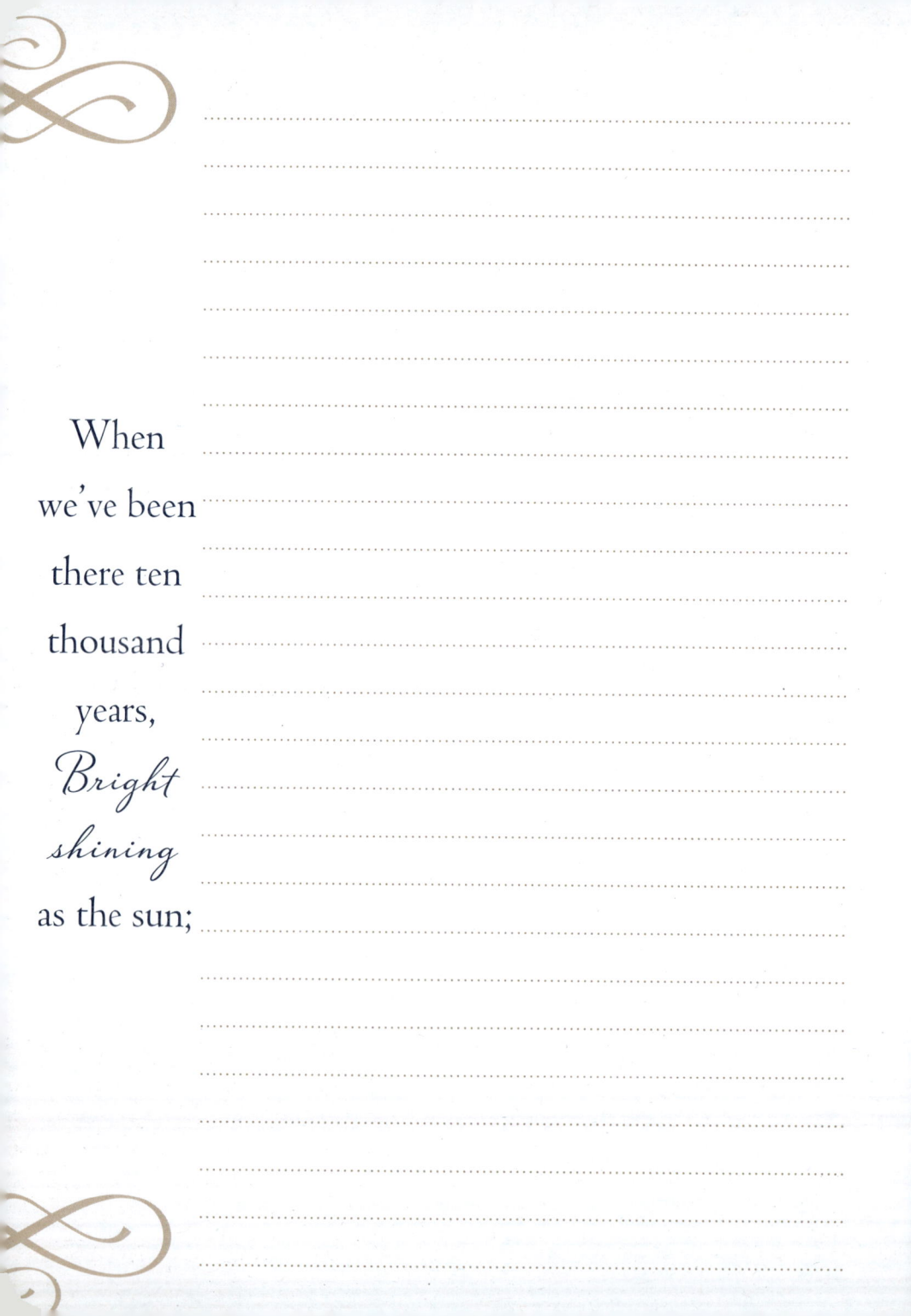

When
we've been
there ten
thousand
years,
Bright
shining
as the sun;

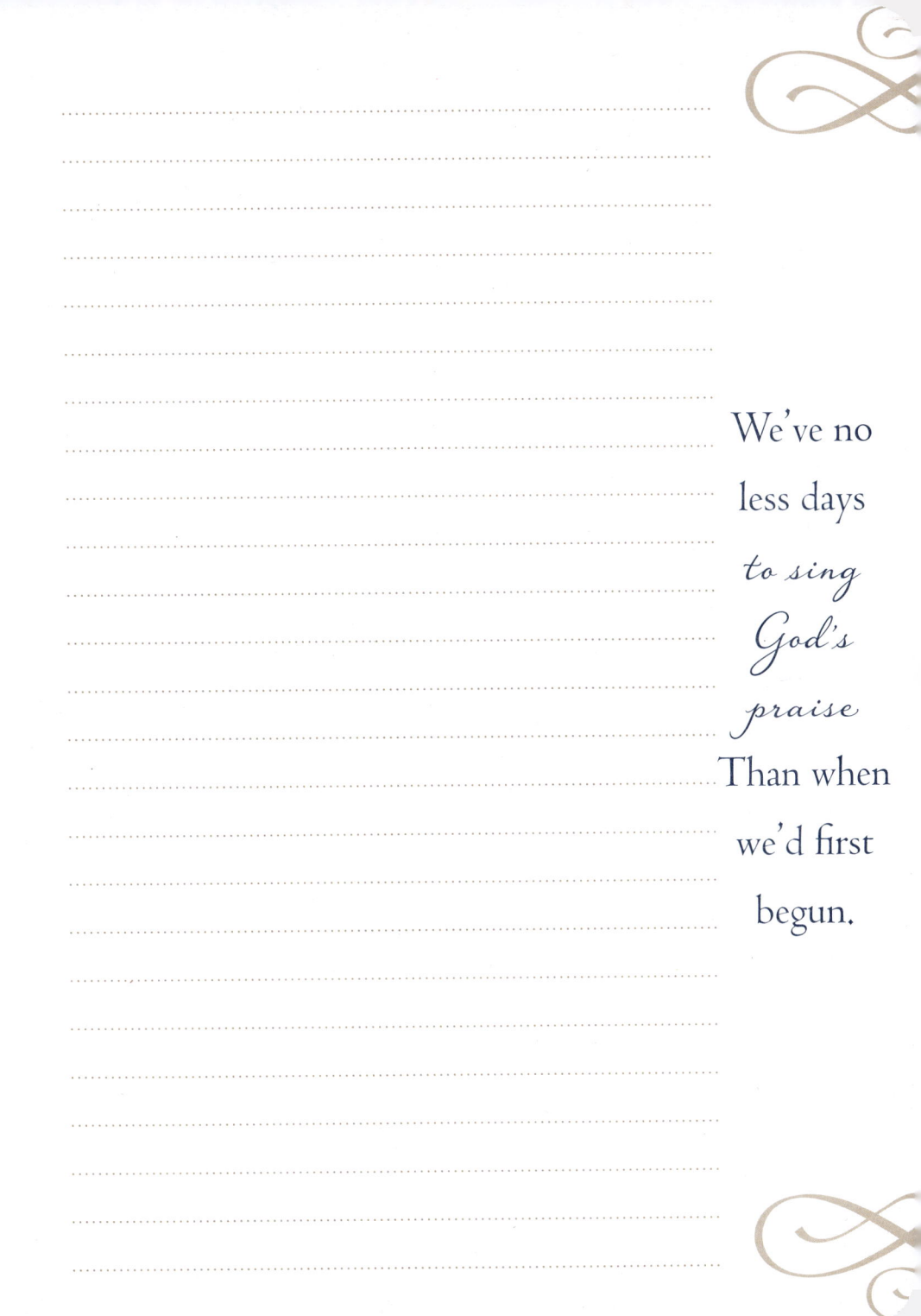

We've no less days to sing God's praise Than when we'd first begun.

Amazing grace, how sweet the sound, That saved a wretch like me!

> I once *was lost* but now am found, *Was blind* but now I see.

'Twas grace that taught my heart to fear, And grace my fears relieved;

How *precious* did that *grace* appear
The hour *I first believed!*

Through many dangers, toils, and snares, I have already come;

> 'Twas *grace* that brought me safe thus far, *And grace* will lead me home.

The Lord has promised good to me. His Word my hope secures.

He will my shield and portion be, As long as life endures.

The earth
shall soon
dissolve
like snow,
The sun
forbear
to shine;

But God, who called me here below, Will be forever mine.

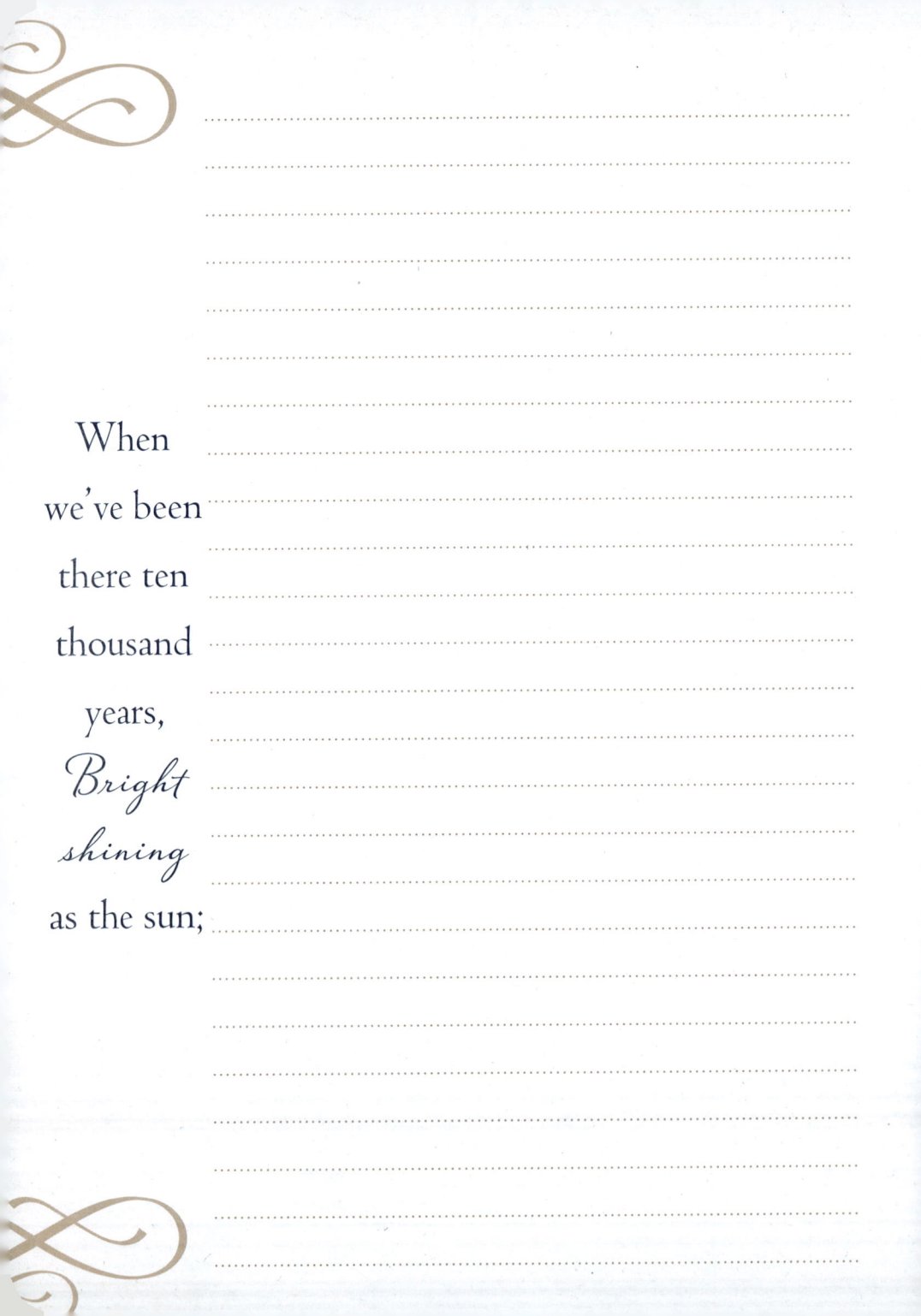

When
we've been
there ten
thousand
years,
Bright
shining
as the sun;

We've no less days to sing God's praise Than when we'd first begun.

Amazing grace, how sweet the sound, That saved a wretch like me!

I once was lost but now am found, Was blind but now I see.

'Twas grace that taught my heart to fear, And grace my fears relieved;

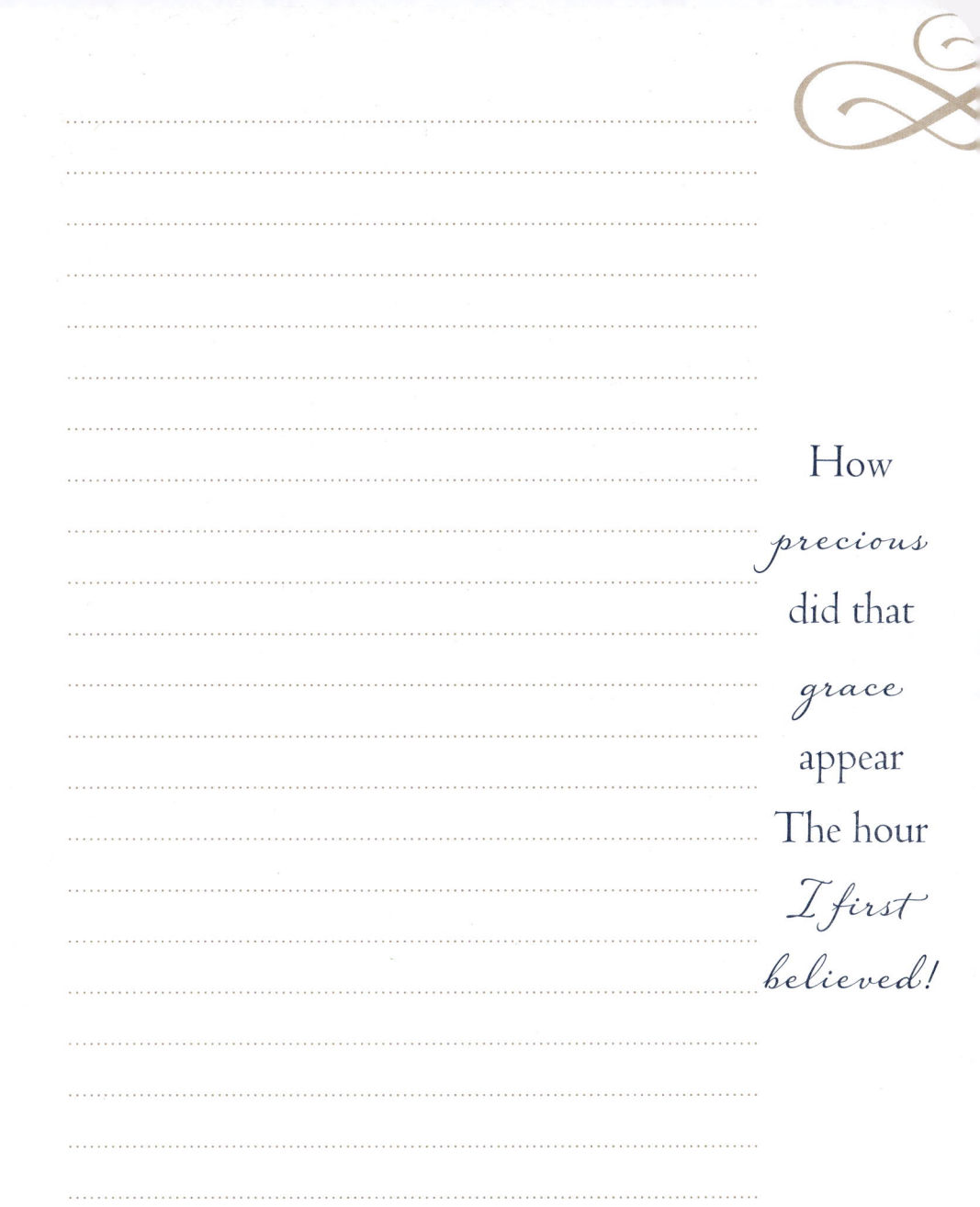

How *precious* did that *grace* appear The hour *I first believed!*

Through many dangers, toils, and snares, I have already come;

'Twas *grace* that brought me safe thus far, *And* *grace* will lead me home.

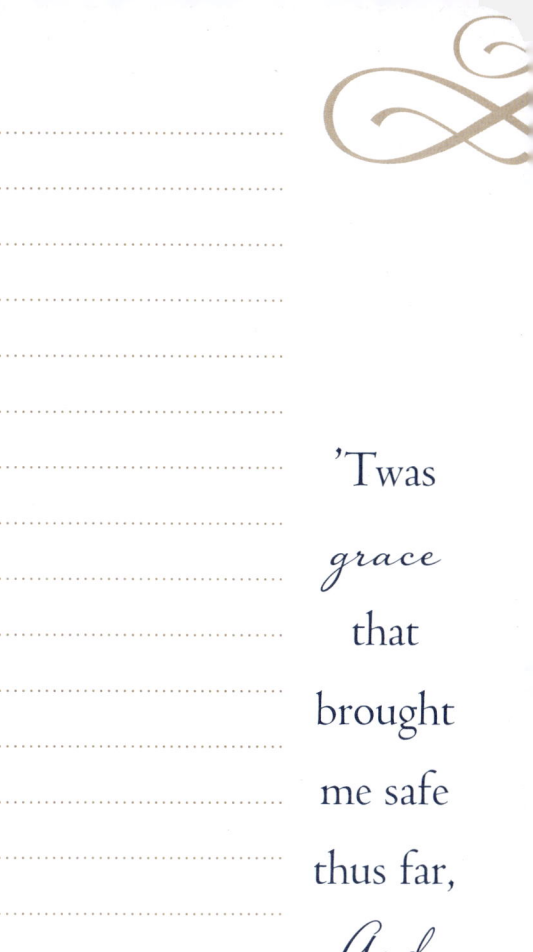

The Lord has promised good to me. His Word my hope secures.

He will my shield and portion be, As long as life endures.

Amazing Grace,
    how sweet the sound
That saved
    a wretch like me,
I once was lost
but now am found,
        Was Blind,
but now I see.

— John Newton